When Demons Attack

True Tales of Diabolic Encounters

John Harker

Some names, locations, and similar identifying details have been changed to protect the identities of the individuals who were either witnesses to or victims of these phenomena.

Table of Contents

Introduction

The Nature of Demons and Demonic Activity

What is a demon and why does it want to attack us?

First, it's important to know that one of the most common shared beliefs among the world's diverse religions and cultures is the belief in demonic spirits, their ability to haunt and possess, and the need for rituals to cast them out of the people and places where they have chosen to take up residence and cause trouble. The most common understanding of demons for those of us in the West is that they are spiritual beings of an angelic nature. In other words, fallen angels. They rebelled against the sovereignty of God and aligned themselves with Lucifer, their leader, who tradition famously ascribes as saying "Non serviam," or, "I will not serve." As their punishment, they were cast from Heaven to earth, where they roam in search of victims for their hate and vindictiveness.

Now, of course, there are variations to this story depending on the culture or creed describing it. But the essential struggle between good and evil is the same despite the differences in the details. For the purposes of this book, a traditional Judeo-Christian concept of demonology is most frequently invoked, primarily because there is an overwhelming amount of academic and anecdotal literature and case studies that offer evidence of its legitimacy.

What is the nature of demons, then? Accepting that demons are fallen angels, we accept that there exists a hierarchy of demonic spirits just as there is a hierarchy of angelic spirits. There are superior ones and inferior ones. In addition to their ranking, they have retained their particular angelic intellect and power, but it has now become twisted and perverse. So, for example, a rebellious angel who was created to encourage chastity is likely now to be a demon of lust.

Demons belong to a preternatural world parallel to that of mankind. The preternatural power that demons possess is far superior to anything humans exercise in the natural world. They can manipulate physical matter, for example, in order to move objects, cause frightening manifestations, or even affect the weather in specific locations. They can also manipulate psychic abilities and even cause certain psychic phenomena such as telepathy, telekinesis, and astral projection.

Nonetheless, their powers are limited. Though they can do things that go beyond the material world, and beyond our imagination, they cannot act beyond their angelic nature. So while God can create something from nothing, a demon cannot. And most importantly, no matter what powers a demon possesses, it can never control or directly interfere with the moral behavior of a human being. Our free will always supersedes.

The next question: Why the hate against humans? Why bother us at all? Father Gary Thomas, an exorcist in California who has dealt with his fair share of demons, explains it this way: "There's a parasitic quality to their existence because they are all slowly dying—they've been dying since the moment they rebelled against God, and so they often times are attaching themselves to artificially experience life, but their ultimate goal is to take many of us into eternal damnation. Because of their jealousy and envy about the human race, they see us as competition, even though they're of a higher nature."

Dr. Richard Gallagher, an academic psychiatrist and author of the book *Demonic Foes*, describes demons as "cosmic terrorists," whose hatred of God drives them to do terrible deeds toward those creatures who reflect the image of the divine, namely, humans. Gallagher goes on to say that because the demonic world has lost its capacity to love in its rejection of God, it now seeks "to negate our loving personalities, destroy us spiritually, and, if it can, even cause our physical death."

If this sounds like we are in a war with an invisible enemy, it's because, in a sense, we are. *Ordinary* demonic attacks happen all the time. If you are a Christian, you are no doubt familiar with the concept of temptation, wherein the devil tries to compel a human into sinful activity by exciting the imagination or igniting the baser levels of the soul. Similarly, Muslims are ever vigilant against the whisperings of the shaitans, beings of hell-fire, who strive to lead humans astray with their evil suggestions. Even in the literature of Buddhism, villainous tempters appear, the most famous being the demon Mara, who challenged the Buddha during his quest for enlightenment, trying at one point to seduce the man with his own daughters.

But then there are the *extraordinary* demonic attacks. These generally fall into three categories: infestation, oppression/obsession, and possession. Infestation is the presence of demons in a specific location. This is the beginning phase of diabolical activity and is characterized by certain classic "haunting" signs: tapping, scratching, or pounding noises on walls and doors; growling or other strange animal-like noises; whispers, cries, screams, laughter—all without a discernible source; bad odors, often of rotting flesh or sulfur; electrical irregularities such as flickering lights; sudden gusts of winds and unexplained cold spots; disappearing objects which are either never found or found in strange, improbable places; damage to religious items; pets suddenly becoming spooked for no apparent reason; and black shadows that glide along floors, walls, and ceilings.

Possible reasons for infestations may include occult activity such as séances, Ouija board usage, and black magic rituals; heinous crimes such as murder or sexual abuse; suicides; curses on the residents or previous residents; or any other number of past actions by a person with authority over the site. Bearing all this in mind, it is a good practice to have a home blessed by a religious figure before moving in.

Oppression and obsession are generally defined as extraordinary demonic attacks against a person. The attacks can be physical, psychological, or both. Physical attacks may include scratching, pushing, choking, biting, burning, and blows that leave bruises, bloody sores, and even bone fractures. Some victims have experienced incisions and marks on their skin in the form of letters, words, and symbols, which manifest for a time and then disappear as mysteriously as they appeared. Psychological attacks may come in the form of persistent, repetitive nightmares and sleep deprivation; obsessive, irrational thoughts; and suicidal or homicidal compulsions. Sometimes the oppression, or *vexation*, as some exorcists call it, will target the victim's health, finances, relationships, or work, causing further stress, pain, and despair.

It is not uncommon in cases of oppression to see manifestations of demons either as a shadow, a black mist, or a hooded figure. As the person enters more deeply into a relationship with the demon, its visage is apt to become more revealed—and more horrific. One possessed person who had a direct vision of demons described them to his exorcist as thus: "They were distorted and misshapen.... Some had claws instead of hands . . . if they had two eyes or any recognizable limbs, they were malformed . . . these demons were all like naked, ugly, vicious animals." Horror movies, he added, do not even come close. Another victim described his tormentor as appearing as a "grotesque, impish figure," while yet other people see the manifestations in the form of cats, crows, and spiders.

Oppression occurs when a person has opened a doorway to the demonic, either knowingly or not. Engaging in occult activities is the primary way to attract demons, and it often comes about in incremental stages. For example, a person uses a Ouija board and makes contact with a "spirit" they believe to be a dead relative. Only the spirit is a demon disguising itself as a non-threatening entity in order to gain the trust of its intended victim. Once a relationship is established, the demon gains more "rights" to the victim due to this consensual interaction. Eventually, the demon gains enough rights to the victim where it doesn't need consent anymore, and this is when it begins to inflict distress.

Demonic attachments don't always happen this way, of course. Many factors determine the nature of the oppression, including the strength of the demon and the vulnerability of the victim. In addition to partaking in the occult, other causes of vexation can include consorting with mediums and fortune tellers, participating in "ghost hunts" and other paranormal investigations, living in a demonically-infested house, having close contact with a possessed person, being the victim of a recent or ancestral curse, and indulging in an immoral, unrepentant lifestyle.

Possession is the final, most frightening, and, thankfully, rarest phase of demonic activity. It occurs in one of two ways: 1) a person voluntarily cooperates with the occult or demonic forces; 2) another person actively cooperating with demonic power brings it to bear on an involuntary victim. In essence, a possession must originate either from a person opening the door to the devil or being a victim of one who has opened that door.

As demonologist and exorcism expert Adam Blai explains, full possession occurs "when a person makes an informed, free choice to give demons the rights to control a body that person has authority over." Note that according to this definition, it's possible not only to give up one's own body to a demon but to offer someone else's, such as the case of a parent offering up their child in a perverse satanic ritual. It is also important to understand that while the demon, or demons (oftentimes there are more than one), resides in the body of a human being during possession, it never "possesses" the person's soul, nor does it completely take over its victim's free will. Their free will may be debilitated, however, and for this reason, a possessed person cannot be held responsible for their words and actions during the periods when the demon emerges and takes over their physicality.

Present in almost every possession is a trance-like state during which the victim's eyes roll back in their head and an alternate personality emerges, one that is filled with arrogance, vulgarity, hatred, and violence. Other classic signs of possession include superhuman strength and unnatural bodily contortions; knowledge of languages the person has never studied; knowledge of hidden information; and a strong aversion to the sacred (churches, holy water, crucifixes, sacred texts, and so forth).

Adam Blai adds an additional sign that is seen on occasion: levitation. "The most common form seems to be when the body rises off the floor and floats six to ten inches off the ground, gliding across the room and moving like a snake." Various other forms of levitation include floating straight up into the air, moving up a wall, sticking to a wall, or "walking" on walls and ceilings.

Poltergeist activity is also common in the presence of a possessed person: doors slamming, objects flying across the room, furniture moving about, footprints appearing on the floor. Sometimes there occurs the appearance of dark figures, animals, insects, and other apparitions.

While telepathy, the ability to read the mind and communicate with remote individuals, has been observed for centuries in cases of the possessed, in modern times demons communicate like so many of us, by cell phone. Father José Francisco Syquia, chief exorcist of the Archdiocese of Manila, says receiving text messages from demons is an experience common to priests helping possessed persons liberate themselves. "Usually [the demons] would swear at you or say, 'This person will never get away from us.'" In one memorable encounter, Father Syquia was counseling a possessed woman (an ex-satanist) when the priest began receiving texts from the woman's phone, which was in another room. "Don't believe Father," read one, while another called the priest a liar and a sinner who wouldn't be able to help. Although the possessed woman only spoke Filipino, additional texts came through that cursed Father Syquia with the very understandable English phrase, "F*ck you."

* * *

Such is the nature of the creatures you'll read about in the following pages. They are not slick-tongued sin salesmen whispering in people's ears, but rather savage and sinister beasts who want to destroy their victims in body and soul. They are intelligent, manipulative, and vile. And despite what some today might think, they are real. The victims whose stories are told in this book learned that all too well. Their encounters are tangible, visceral, and terrifying.

The purpose of this book is not to frighten (though that may occur), but to shed light on the various ways demons operate in our world and to offer hope in their defeat. Some of the stories are short, some are long. Each brings a unique set of circumstances and perspective to a dark yet fascinating area of study. Though the manifestations described may differ in degree and form, all should serve to give us pause about the world around us: that which we can see and that which we cannot.

"They do enjoy conflict, pain, chaos and breaking families apart. They relish all of that. They enjoy that. They just find it pleasurable. They're very sadistic creatures."

– Adam Blai, religious demonologist and advisor
for the Diocese of Pittsburgh

The Demon Under the House

Kevin and Holly Flynn clutched their rosaries fervently with one hand while reaching for each other with their other. As they knelt on the floor, their backs to the parlor door, they struggled to recite the prayers they knew by heart and which on any other day would escape their lips like water from an open tap. But on this day, at this hour, the scene in front of them was so surreal that they could hardly think straight or breathe right, let alone talk.

There was, however, someone talking in the room, a strange man with a sickly pallor who only twenty minutes earlier had invited himself into their house to help the couple with their "predicament." He was talking loudly and in a language neither Kevin nor Holly recognized. Seated with the man, who called himself Higgins, were three young women dressed in Bohemian-style clothing. As Higgins continued his bizarre monologue, the women chanted nondescript words while swaying trance-like in their chairs.

Kevin and Holly knew the odd foursome weren't praying—not in the same sense, at least, that they were—as Higgins told them at the outset, "We don't pray. We connect." Though the Flynns tried to focus on the prayer beads wound around their fingers, they couldn't help but wonder what exactly Higgins was trying to connect to. It didn't take long before they had an answer.

Amid the verbal chaos taking place, a rumbling sound began under the sofa against the far wall. The sound intensified, and as it did it took on a physical manner, moving out from under the sofa toward the center of the room. The floorboards vibrated as the "something" rolled under the kneeling Flynns and under the feet of Higgins and his crew, who appeared nonplussed while continuing their lingual onslaught. The undulating mass pushed on across the room, went out under the door, and disappeared into the hall.

Kevin and Holly had experienced their fair share of disturbing events over the past year, but nothing like what they just witnessed. What monstrous entity had Higgins just unleashed on them? Hadn't he said he came to help? Though terrified beyond reason, they found their voices and began praying again in earnest. But the louder they prayed, the more Higgins raised his voice, drowning them out in that strange language, his inflection reaching a crescendo until, suddenly, he stopped. The Flynns stopped as well. An eerie quiet fell upon the room.

"Our guest in the hallway wishes to come in now," Higgins said, his voice level and calm. He turned and looked directly at the Flynns. "You don't have to look at it if you don't want to. If that's what you choose, it would be best to keep your eyes closed."

At those words, Kevin and Holly went into shock. As Kevin would later recall, they were so filled with fear that they couldn't move, they couldn't speak, they couldn't pray. "All we could do was shut our eyes tight and wait."

* * *

The "predicament" that the mysterious Higgins had referred to began about a year earlier on June 10, 2004, when Kevin and Holly, along with their two young children, Cara and Sean, moved into their new house on Ireland's rugged west coast in a rural part of County Galway. Situated in the shadow of the Twelve Pins mountain range, the house had been built from the ground up over a long-demolished cottage that had belonged to Kevin's uncles. The two uncles, who had never married, had lived together in the cottage for well over forty years before dying within weeks of each other. Much to the surprise of family members, they bequeathed their modest house and the twenty acres of farmland it sat upon to neighbors. Kevin's father, a brother to the men, vowed to someday buy the land back but died before he could. Kevin was therefore overjoyed when the opportunity came about for him to buy the land, for not only did it provide a new and bigger living space for his young family, but it allowed him to reclaim the patch of land that had for generations belonged to the Flynns.

Settling into a new home is an experience often beset with challenges and imbued with peculiarities. The Flynns found this to be true right away. On the very first day of unpacking, Holly couldn't shake a feeling of unease when she was in one particular room, the small parlor to the right of the front door. It had a coldness to it at odds with the rest of the house, and on more than one occasion, Holly found herself looking over her shoulder, certain someone was there with her, only to see no one. Shaking it off as new house jitters, she continued putting things in place in the parlor, including a family Bible which she placed on a shelf above the fireplace. As she was still facing the fireplace, she heard the soft click of the door closing behind her.

"Kevin, is that you?"

Receiving no answer, she rushed over to open the door. No one was in sight. In the kitchen she found Kevin, who denied closing the door. Maybe the wind had blown it shut, he suggested. Or maybe it was just a new house glitch. Maybe, Holly thought to herself. But all the windows were closed and there were no trees moving outside. A glitch, perhaps, but that didn't explain the unmistakable feeling she remembered of someone, or something, entering the room when that door had closed.

The next couple of months found the Flynns becoming more comfortable with their new surroundings while learning to navigate their busy lives. With small children, the household could often become chaotic, so when little items like keys and cups started going missing or the telephone receiver seemed to always be knocked off the hook, Holly and Kevin either blamed each other or the kids. But as Christmas neared, something happened that was harder to blame on anyone. Three mornings in a row, Holly found the family Bible off its shelf and lying in the middle of the parlor floor. Bizarrely, it was always opened to the same page: Isaiah 28.

And then there was the matter of Michael.

As was Kevin's custom, each night when he tucked three-year-old Sean into bed he would check for the boogeyman under the boy's bed. On one particular night, Kevin did his perfunctory check and then declared, "Nope, no boogeyman."

"But the boogeyman isn't down there, Daddy," Sean replied, his eyes turned toward the other side of the room. "He's by the window."

"Well, I'll throw him out the window, then," Kevin said as he started over that way.

"Never mind, Daddy. He just went through the wall."

Sean seemed at ease, so Kevin chuckled inwardly at his son's imagination, kissed him goodnight, and thought no more of the matter. Over the next several nights, the same scenario played out at bedtime: Kevin would check for the boogeyman under the bed, Sean would insist he was by the window, and then the "monster" would disappear into a wall. After about a week, Sean told Kevin that he didn't have to check for the boogeyman anymore because, he announced, "Michael comes in and sends him away."

"Oh?" said Kevin, smiling. "Who's Michael?"

"He has wings and he sits on the roof. After you leave, he comes in and sends the bad man away."

Kevin considered Sean's story as simply an addition to the fantasy he'd been indulging in the last couple of weeks. It wouldn't be until some months later when, coupled with other astonishing and terrifying paranormal events, Kevin decided Sean wasn't imagining things.

* * *

It was Christmas of that year when, as Kevin described it, "all hell broke loose." Holly's parents had spent the day with them, exchanging gifts and celebrating merrily. After they had left, Kevin and Holly tucked the kids in bed, watched a movie, and then retired to their bedroom around eleven. Shortly after falling asleep, they were awakened by loud knocking on the front door. Holly thought maybe her parents had returned. The knocking intensified as Kevin scrambled downstairs.

"Hang on, hang on, I'm coming," he yelled.

He flung the door open, expecting to see perhaps a stranded motorist if not his in-laws, but was stunned when he saw . . . no one. Not only was no one on the steps, but there were no footprints or tire tracks in the freshly-fallen snow anywhere Kevin could see. Holly soon joined him at the door, looking equally perplexed. Just then more knocking ensued, this time at the back door. They closed the front and started toward the back. Before they got there, the knocking ceased . . . and then resumed back at the front door, this time louder and more insistent.

Kevin and Holly looked at each other and knew what the other was thinking: they were dealing with something supernatural. The knocking continued unabated, switching between the front and back doors, as if an army of knuckles was conducting synchronized rapping drills. Too terrified to move, Kevin and Holly stood in the hallway close together, praying that whatever was out there remained outside. Suddenly the knocking stopped. "It's over," whispered Holly. Emboldened by the peaceful quiet, the couple slowly inched their way back up the stairs. They had almost made it to the top when they heard a noise that made their blood run cold — the creaking of the front door opening. They watched in disbelief as the door swung all the way open, letting an icy blast of air sweep into the house.

Kevin tried to be nonchalant. "It was the wind. I forgot to lock it." He started down the stairs to close the door, but before he reached the bottom, the door swung shut by itself. And then began a sound Kevin and Holly will never forget—the unmistakable sound of heavy footsteps walking across the hall toward the staircase. Toward them.

They ran to their bedroom and locked themselves in. Holly collapsed on the bed, sobbing. Kevin continued to listen to the thud of the footsteps growing louder as they came up the stairs. At the top of the landing, they stopped for just a moment, then headed in the direction of Sean's and Cara's rooms. His fatherly instinct overriding his terror, Kevin raced out into the corridor. It was empty. He and Holly checked on the children and found them blissfully asleep, though how they could sleep through all that racket remained a mystery. They blessed Sean and Cara with holy water they kept on a windowsill, returned to their own room, knelt down, and immediately began to pray a rosary. They were halfway through when Holly exclaimed, "I heard something. Outside the window. Listen!"

Moments later Kevin heard it too: the unmistakable wail of a woman in agony. They looked out the window but could see no one outside. They resumed their prayer, but the ghostly moaning only got louder, no matter how much the Flynns raised their voices in an attempt to drown it out. When rapping started on their bedroom window, the Flynns gave up, and for the next several hours they simply endured the onslaught of nonstop moaning, screaming, and knocking. At 3:00 a.m., Kevin finally called his mother and sister and asked them to come over. He needed witnesses to the insanity going on in his house. He didn't need to persuade his mother much—she could hear the commotion through the phone line.

Kevin's mother and sister arrived at 4:00 and were immediately immersed in the nightmare at hand. The woman's wailing was louder than ever, and the knocking was going on at all the doors and windows. Amazingly, the children continued to sleep like rocks throughout the nightmarish ordeal. The family gathered in the parlor and began another rosary together. Fittingly, as it had done time and time again, the Bible flew down from its shelf and landed yet again with its pages open to Isaiah 28.

At 4:30 a.m., the bedlam abruptly stopped. The house became as quiet as the outside snowfall, and everyone present breathed multiple sighs of relief.

"You need to call a priest," Kevin's mother stated matter-of-factly.

* * *

Father Bartley arrived the next day and wasted no time in blessing the house. He speculated that it could be a wandering soul—or souls, maybe more than one—that could be responsible for the disturbances. Perhaps the trouble came from Kevin's uncles, who were still "trapped" in the place in which they died. He urged the Flynns to pray for the uncles' souls and to bid them goodbye.

That night, Kevin and Holly went to bed feeling reassured by the priest's visit. Exhausted by the events of the last 24 hours, they began to fall asleep almost immediately when, minutes later, they were awakened by the heart-stopping sound of a door being opened across the hall—the door to Sean's room, which Holly knew she had closed right before coming to bed. The couple raced out to the hall and cautiously pushed open their son's door, which had indeed been opened a crack. The room was completely empty—no intruder, but also no Sean.

"Maybe he went into Cara's room," Kevin said. They turned to check when Holly spotted something that made her cry out. She raced down the stairs where Sean lay at the bottom, curled up in a ball and sleeping as peacefully as in a fairy tale. Even as she carried him back to his bed, he never once woke up, his calm, gentle breathing mocking Holly's own distressed ventilation. The couple once again blessed him with holy water before retiring back to their bedroom. No sooner had they settled in when they heard a loud pounding on the front door. A minute later, screams echoed outside their window. Father Bartley's blessing had apparently been for naught. The Flynns were again under siege by unseen forces, but his time Kevin and Holly weren't going to wait it out. They packed some necessities, bundled up the children, and drove to Kevin's mother's house.

Kevin kept his family at his mom's house through New Year's and then called Father Bartley again. The priest came back to the Flynns' home, this time accompanied by a visiting missionary. Together the clergymen did an extensive blessing of each room in the house, with prayers said in both English and Latin. Though not a formal exorcism, the blessing seemed to work. For three weeks, the Flynns enjoyed a peace they hadn't know since moving in.

And then the trouble started again.

At first, it was little disturbances: objects out of place, lights flickering, the Bible falling to the floor (still opening to Isaiah). But then one night Kevin woke up and saw a tall, hooded figure standing in the corner of the room. Its face was obscured in the shadows of the hood, and its arms were crossed over its chest, hands hidden in the folds of its garment. Kevin woke Holly, who cried out immediately upon seeing the intruder. They shouted at it to go away, but it wouldn't move, even when they turned on a light. Kevin and Holly weren't as immobile; they raced across the room, threw open the door, and were shocked to see the same black-hooded figure standing at the bottom of the stairs. Quickly, they gathered Sean and Cara (both of whom remained asleep throughout the disturbance) and carried them back to their bedroom. Their adrenalin running high and fear running even higher, they slept little that night, but thankfully the mysterious entity did not reappear.

In the morning they called Father Bartley, and for the third time the priest arrived with the sincere intention of putting to rest whatever was plaguing the Flynns. He offered Mass in the parlor without incident and then sat with the Flynns to talk some more over tea. It was at this point that Sean, who was normally very shy and never approached visitors, tugged at Father Bartley's sleeve and in a most serious manner said, "Michael put the bad man in the fire."

"In that fire there?" the priest asked, pointing to the fireplace.

"No, the big fire down there." Sean bent down and touched his fingers to the rug.

Looking perplexed, Father Bartley then asked Sean, "How did Michael do that, Sean?"

"With his big sword." And with that, Sean left the room.

Kevin immediately remembered the conversation he had had with Sean months earlier about "Michael." He recounted that episode to Father Bartley and also told him that while he and Holly had taught their children the basics of Catholicism, they couldn't remember ever having spoken about St. Michael the Archangel, nor did they have any pictures in the house depicting the angelic warrior. The priest nodded, looking a bit paler than before. He told the Flynns he would be back that evening with some "special prayers" that he had never had to use before. He explained to them, "Children are very sensitive to the 'invisible world.' That's why I'm worried about what Sean said."

Father Bartley arrived back at 6:00 p.m. and gathered Kevin and Holly into the parlor. He gave them prayer sheets and instructed them to follow along and to recite the lines he had highlighted. He also told them to ignore anything that might "happen" and to keep praying. Then they knelt and began. It wasn't more than a few minutes into the session, at the reading of Psalm 53, that the Flynn's Bible fell off its shelf. But this time, instead of landing face up to the passage in Isaiah, the pages in the book began to turn themselves from right to left as if being riffled by invisible fingers. Though Kevin and Holly were astonished at the sight in front of them, Father Bartley ignored it and continued his recitation.

Suddenly the priest paused and peered intently at the sofa along the back wall, his hands that held the prayer book shaking ever so slightly. Kevin and Holly could tell that something—something they couldn't see—had caught Father Bartley's attention. Just then, a loud rumble emanated from beneath the sofa and a vibration rippled through the floor that nearly knocked the three of them over. Looking over at the Flynns, the priest instructed them to continue their responses, then went and stood before the sofa. His voice faltering just a touch, he resumed his prayers even as another tremor pulsated from beneath the couch.

Terrified, Kevin and Holly increased the fervor of their prayer, their intention now focused on finishing quickly and bolting from the room. They feared for Father Bartley; the priest was becoming noticeably unsteady as he alternated between staring at the sofa and reading from his prayer book. Should they go to him? they wondered. But just then, the priest was flung backward into an armchair as if someone had aggressively pushed him. He scrambled to his feet, waving back Kevin and Holly who were about to rush to him. "I'm fine," he said. "Keep kneeling. I need to finish this."

Once again the priest positioned himself in front of the sofa, and once again he was thrown back into the armchair. This time he stood where he was. In a cracking voice, he resumed, "God and Lord of all creation! Grant me constant faith and power, so that armed with the power of your holy strength, I can attack this cruel evil spirit—"

Father Bartley's prayer book suddenly lifted from his grasp and fell to the floor. The priest slumped into the chair behind him and said in a defeated voice, "I'm sorry. I can't do this."

Kevin and Holly brought Father Bartley to the kitchen and restored their nerves with glasses of brandy. While never saying exactly what he saw by the sofa, Father Bartley did ask Kevin if there were any remnants of his uncles' old cottage in the parlor. Kevin thought for a moment, and then remembered that, indeed, there had been an issue with the old hearthstone. It had been too heavy to move, so they had decided to just build over it.

Father Bartley nodded and then said, almost to himself, "That's where it lives."

"Where what lives?" asked Kevin

The priest ignored the question and told Kevin that what the house needed was an exorcism. He himself was not qualified to perform one, but he would talk to the bishop about arranging for an exorcist to visit the Flynns as soon as possible. In the meantime, he advised, continue to pray daily and liberally sprinkle holy water throughout the home.

For two weeks the Flynns experienced a disturbance-free existence. But then all manner of manifestations started up again: the incessant knocking on the doors and windows; the wailings and moanings of a phantom woman in the middle of the night; the appearance of the black hooded figure in Kevin and Holly's bedroom; and, as if that wasn't enough, one morning finding that the framed pictures of Cara and Sean in the parlor had been turned around to face the wall.

The Flynns were on the verge of moving out when one morning Kevin received a puzzling phone call at work. The caller identified himself as a Mr. Higgins and offered to help Kevin with his "predicament," or to be more exact, to help "where others have failed." Kevin wondered if this was the exorcist promised by Father Bartley, but when asked, the caller chuckled and said no, but that he nonetheless comes with a "special blessing." Dismissing Kevin's preference to trust in the Church ("Your church is not getting any results now, is it?"), Higgins told him he would come around at a time of his choosing and then abruptly hung up.

Kevin sat holding the phone, perplexed. He decided to keep the call to himself, as he felt it likely was a hoax and there was no point in upsetting Holly any further.

The next evening, however, after he and Holly had finished dinner, the mystery caller showed up at his door.

"Ronan Higgins," the visitor said as he held a hand out to Kevin. "We spoke on the phone yesterday."

"Ah, yes, but I thought I told you I wasn't interested—" Kevin began but lost his choice of words when Higgins and his entourage of three young women pushed past him and made their way down the hall to the parlor.

"What the hell! I didn't invite you in," exclaimed Kevin.

"No, you didn't. But you need me, Mr. Flynn." The three women set about closing the curtains in the room and arranging chairs in a semi-circle. "This room is where it lives."

By now Holly had joined the fray. "I'm calling the police," she said.

Higgins turned and looked at the Flynns with an icy stare. "If you do that, you'll be worse off than you were before. I am here to calm the evil that resides here. At the behest of your uncles."

"My uncles? How do you know them? They've been dead for ages."

"Well, you see, Mr. Flynn, I talk to the dead. And two nights ago I received a message from them directing me to this property. Now, shall we get on with it? I really am here to help."

Numbly, Kevin nodded in agreement. "We pray first, though," he managed.

Higgins chuckled and said, "If you like. It won't do any good, but it won't interfere with our doings."

Kevin and Holly clutched their rosaries and began: "I believe in God the Father Almighty . . . ."

* * *

"Our guest in the hallway wishes to come in now."

As they waited on their knees, eyes closed tightly and paralyzed with fear, Kevin and Holly felt the air around them turn bone-chillingly cold. They heard Higgins give a mysterious command toward the direction of the door, then, the sound of the door slowly opening.

They knew instantly that something—the "guest"—was in the doorway. And it was accompanied by the vilest odor Kevin had ever encountered. He felt sick and wanted to run out of the room, but that would have meant opening his eyes and having to run past whatever monstrosity was in the room with them. Even without his sight, he could sense that the entity was massive. Along with its stench, it also *rustled*, as if it had wings. "I now know that it was . . . that it was a demon," Kevin later reported.

Higgins started speaking to it in that strange, arcane language he had been using before. Incredibly, the *thing* answered back in a similar fashion. Kevin and Holly recalled later how the voice was that of a man, very deep but discarnate, never coming from one fixed place but rather from all over the room. The chattering grew louder and more intense as if the two were arguing. And then, abruptly, the deep male voice spoke loudly in English.

"Give me what I want!"

"No!" snapped Higgins. "You can't have him."

"I will not leave until I have him!"

Higgins reverted back to the mystery language and engaged once again in a vociferous exchange with the intruder for several minutes before finally commanding in English: "Now return to your pit!"

Kevin and Holly felt something swish by them, accompanied by a loud rumbling that traveled past them under the floor and ended by the sofa on the far wall. Silence descended on the room. The Flynns slowly felt their postures thaw and their breathing return to normal as the coldness and the stench gradually dissipated. Higgins's three assistants busied themselves opening the curtains and putting chairs back in their places.

"What the hell was that?" Kevin demanded, rising to his feet and glaring at Higgins.

"That, Mr. Flynn, was an evil spirit that's been living in this house for a very long time. It has no intention of leaving, and your prayers and your silly clergymen are useless against it. When they come around, it simply hides in its pit under the hearthstone."

The hearthstone. That's where Father Bartley said it lives, too.

"So, what, it wants the house? It wants us to leave?"

"Oh, it wants very much more than that. It wants your soul, Mr. Flynn."

Kevin looked at him aghast. He opened his mouth to speak, but Higgins cut him off.

"It's why your uncles didn't bequeath this property to your father. But then you had to go and upset their wishes, didn't you? It's never a good idea, Mr. Flynn, to meddle in the affairs of the dead."

"So…so what do we do now?"

"I suggest you sell this place and move away at once. I've bought you some time, but I'm afraid that's all I can do. It wants you, Mr. Flynn, and it will take you eventually if you stay. The choice is simple: leave or risk damnation. Good day now, sir."

Kevin watched in confusion and shock as Higgins and his crew drove off his property as mysteriously as they had arrived. His reverie was short-lived, broken by a crash within the house. He hurried down the hall and found Holly in the small sitting room across from the parlor. Together they looked in dismay at the broken remains of a crucifix that had been hanging on one of the walls. Just then a second crash emanated from the parlor. This time it was a framed picture of Christ's

Sacred Heart that had fallen from the wall and now lay in a heap of shattered glass.

Enough was enough. The Flynns packed up and moved out.

* * *

Father Andrew Sullivan used the Latin version of the *Rituale Romanum*, the Catholic Church's formal rite of exorcism. He believed it to be more effective than English. He would know, as he had been doing exorcisms for over 50 years and had seen more in that time than anyone could imagine. A monk who lived in a cloistered monastery, Father Sullivan only left his community when asked to deal with those cases of demonic activity that had defeated other priests and/or was characterized by a particular nasty anti-religious element. The Flynn house, of course, ticked all those boxes.

After completing the exorcism, Father Sullivan reflected on the Flynn case, one of the more unusual ones he had come across. He agreed with the mysterious Higgins that it was indeed an evil spirit—a demon—that had taken possession of the house and not a "restless spirit." But that is all Higgins got right, according to the elderly monk. A devotee of the dark arts, as Higgins undoubtedly was, will only serve to make things worse when he or she attempts to dabble with the demonic. The increased hostility toward the Flynns' religious objects after Higgins left was proof of this, according to Father Sullivan.

As to the origin of the demon, the priest was not so certain. That part of Ireland, Father Sullivan recounted, was a stronghold of the Druids in ages past. Even St. Patrick himself could not convert the tribes that lived there. The evil in the Flynn house could have come about from that time, the priest speculated, given the stories of human sacrifices, cannibalism, and other atrocities committed in that land. "We never know what we're inheriting, do we now?"

There was little doubt that Kevin's uncles knew they were sharing their house with something evil and had resigned themselves to living with the entity for years. Father Sullivan speculated that the uncles were too afraid to tell anyone about their tormentor—either for fear of human ridicule or non-human reprisal—and so chose to deal with it by themselves. It also explained why the property was not bequeathed to any relatives. The uncles were trying to protect their family.

It is hard to fathom how anyone could "deal with" such a terrifying situation for decades without going mad. But somehow Kevin's uncles managed, only showing themselves to be somewhat "eccentric" to family and local townspeople. Everyone knew, for example, that the brothers filled a plastic gallon container with holy water every week at Mass. *Did they cook with it? Drink it?*

Kevin's father finally asked his brother about it on the elder sibling's deathbed. The reply he got he chalked up to the rantings of a dying old man. "We used it for the hearthstone. To put the fire out."

The Rampaging Beast

Charles Gilliam was a man of secrets. Terrible secrets. To those who worked alongside him, Gilliam was a smart and conscientious employee who took his job as an appliance salesman very seriously. To relatives and friends, he was a loving family man who held his wife and kids in the highest esteem. But Gilliam had them all fooled. Behind the veneer of all-around great guy hid a dangerous and depraved man who would do anything for his cloven-footed, horned god, including molesting his own children.

Gilliam was a practicing Satanist. His wife worked nights, leaving him alone with their two young sons and allowing him to participate in vile satanic rituals with his coven. Gilliam's sons were not only victims of sexual molestation at these gatherings, but were also forced to watch the ritualistic killing of small animals. When Gilliam's wife came home early one night and caught them in the act, the coven was disbanded and the police became involved. During the subsequent investigation, detectives unearthed an even more shocking allegation. The coven had supposedly sacrificed a living baby. Although police found the box that the baby had been reportedly buried in, they failed to find an actual body. Gilliam evaded the charge of murder but not of child abuse, and was sentenced to a lengthy prison term.

Gilliam's secrets may have been exposed, but something awful and evil remained hidden in his house. An ancient and cruel entity, summoned by the wickedness of foolish men, waited patiently for its time to act. It just had to wait for the right prey.

* * *

The McGraths loved their new home. They were a large family, and the charming vine-covered colonial on a quiet street in Washington, D.C., seemed perfect for their needs. But tragedy struck a mere three days after they moved in. Frank, father to the three McGrath teenage girls and husband to Judy, found out he had inoperable cancer. He died a month later. The family was devastated, but the girls and Judy knew they had to move forward with their lives. Over the next year, Judy obtained a position as a hotel manager and entered into a new romantic relationship; Ellie, Lisa, and Katie settled into school and made friends; and Judy's niece, Aubrey, came to live with them, adding one more teenager to the mix. All seemed to be going well for the McGraths when, suddenly and without warning, an unimaginable horror turned their world upside down again.

Seventeen-year-old Ellie was the first victim. Her bedroom was in the basement, a large space that was divided into several rooms, including a sitting area with a television and bar. Ellie liked the sense of independence having her room down there gave her. But one night about a week before Christmas, she would have given anything not to be alone. She had been sleeping when she was jarred awake by a raucous pounding on her nightstand. Three violent thumps followed by light rapping, repeated over and over. Ellie was facing away from her table and was too terrified to turn around and look. She thought someone had broken into the house and was about to kill her. Suddenly the pounding stopped, and Ellie felt the presence of someone, or something, right alongside her head, breathing heavily in her ear. Its breath was repulsive and its voice raspy and archaic as it said, "I want to make love to you." Catapulted by fear, Ellie jumped out of bed and ran to her mother's room. As she fled in sheer panic, she did take note of one thing: there was no visible intruder in her room.

Judy tried to assure her daughter that it had just been a nightmare, but Ellie remained adamant that something real, something with intelligence and malice, had been with her that night. Judy chalked it up to the wild imaginings of a teenager and thought nothing more of it for months—until one night the following winter when she experienced her own night of terror.

She had been sleeping for several hours when she was awakened by heavy breathing in her ear. She tried to move away but couldn't budge a finger. She tried to cry out but couldn't utter a sound. The presence beside her emanated pure evil, and Judy thought for sure it was going to kill her. Then, though physically paralyzed, she felt herself falling endlessly, her mind screaming out to God for help. The falling sensation stopped and suddenly Judy was in her living room. But things weren't right. The furniture looked wavy and transparent, and the walls were shimmering with the faces of her children. Judy moved into the kitchen and reached for the phone. She dialed her mother's number, and a male voice answered, "Hello." The voice belonged to Frank, her dead husband. Judy screamed and the next thing she knew she was back in her bed.

Judy's out-of-body experience marked the beginning of a sadistic reign of terror that would leave the McGraths not only questioning their sanity but fearing for their lives. Loud clumping footsteps were heard frequently coming from the basement and usually heralded a terrible event yet to come. A crying baby was another unsettling noise often heard, as was the sound of animal-like growling. Shadowy human-like figures, as well as shapeless black masses, were seen gliding down hallways and passing through doors and walls. One night, Judy's boyfriend, Doug, who now lived with the McGraths, reported hearing crying coming from Lisa's room. He went in to see what was wrong, but no one was in the room. However, on Lisa's bed was a plastic doll with tears running down its face. A doll that was not manufactured to make noise or tears. Another night, Doug woke to use the bathroom and was startled to see what he described as a "monster" with rough fur sticking up all over its body hunkered down in the hall. He watched in amazement as the thing slowly dematerialized in front of his eyes.

Over time, the attacks increased in violence and frequency. One Sunday after church, Judy and her daughters, and Judy's friend Rachel gathered in the McGraths' living room to say some special deliverance prayers Judy's minister had recommended. As they were praying, the youngest, Katie, suddenly complained that her stomach felt on fire. She lifted her shirt and there on her abdomen was a fresh red scratch mark. With renewed fervor, the group resumed praying but was cut short when again Katie yelled out, "Mommy, my face!" As the others looked on, three side-by-side scratch marks appeared on Katie's cheek. A moment later, Rachel cried out as scratch marks appeared on her face, neck, and arms. To Judy it was obvious that the praying had infuriated the "presence" in the house, and she quickly disbanded the group.

The next day Judy's niece, Aubrey, was attacked by the same clawing demon. It raked across her face and arms so hard that she bled. Judy knew she had to do something, so she took the family to her brother's house. But as she quickly discovered, leaving the house didn't make them any safer. "*It followed us*," Judy recalled, "and the children were attacked again." Judy watched in horror as something raked its claws across Katie's face. Not even huddling close, with Judy and Doug acting as shields to the girls, stopped the onslaught. "The kids looked like battered children," Judy told interviewers later.

Feeling defeated and scared, especially now that they knew no place was safe, they returned home the next day. Where, they would soon discover, unthinkable new horrors awaited them.

It targeted Katie again. The girl had said her goodnights and walked into her bedroom when she suddenly stopped short, her mind not fully comprehending what she was seeing. There on her bed lay a monstrous hairy beast, "like Bigfoot," as Katie described it later. It spoke to her inside her mind, saying the most vile and vulgar things. Holding its giant male appendage in one hand, it told her it was going to rape and kill her that night. Then it roared in perverse laughter and vanished in a blink of an eye.

Katie ran from the room in a state of hysteria to her mother. As Judy listened in shock to her sobbing daughter's horrific tale, a weight of despair and helplessness descended upon her. But there was anger too. She stormed into Katie's room and called out: "Please, I'm begging you as a mother, don't take my child tonight! Whatever damnable thing you are, don't hurt my daughter—hurt *me*, if you must!" The reply was a thundering, derisive laugh that shook the house.

Not knowing what else to do, Judy called the Baptist minister who had given her the deliverance prayers. Apologetically, he told her that things had escalated beyond his help and that she needed to call a Catholic priest for an exorcism. Picking the nearest one from the phone book, Judy called and explained everything that had been happening: the footsteps, the crying noises, the growls, the scratches, and now, the lewd threats. The priest listened and then gave her a devastating and heartless answer. Maybe, he told her, this was God's way of getting her back to church. With that, he hung up.

Judy stared at the phone in shock. And fear. If even a man of God wouldn't help her family, then who? Clutching the phone tighter, she called her last lifeline: her mother. "I know it's almost midnight," Judy said in a choked voice, "but we have to come over. It's an emergency." As soon as she had uttered those words, the anguished wail of a baby filled the air, followed by more hideous laughter. Judy's mother, Barbara, was just about to ask what was going on when the cigarette she was smoking was suddenly knocked out of her mouth. As she helplessly watched the cigarette flip through the air, she heard a deafening whistle and the loud thud of something hitting the side of the house. A loud crash followed, and Barbara saw that her favorite sculpture, an angel, had been flung from its shelf and was lying in pieces on the floor. A strange chill went through her, not once but three times. Barbara remarked that each time it felt like the "chill of death."

By now, Judy and Barbara were crying together over the phone, each feeling the immense sadness and despair of not being able to help the other. Unfortunately, their evil oppressor still wasn't done. As Judy listened in horror, her mother's sobs suddenly became desperate, choking gasps. The *thing* was strangling her mother. "I couldn't breathe," the older woman recounted. "I could hear a roaring in my ears and a lot of noise...I thought I was going to die." Just as she thought she was going to pass out, the invisible hands around her throat let go. She slumped back into her chair and reached for a new cigarette with trembling hands. She was okay, she told Judy. Shaken but okay.

Judy knew she couldn't take her kids to her mom's. When Doug came home from work about an hour later, he and Judy and the girls gathered together in one bedroom, Doug guarding the door and Judy huddled on the bed with her daughters and niece. Though terrified on the inside, they took some comfort in the notion of strength in numbers. And since nothing further happened to anyone that night, maybe that was the key. But how long could they keep up such an arrangement? They couldn't do everything together all the time.

Over the course of the next month, the McGraths slowly resumed their normal activities. Though no attacks or other frightening phenomena occurred, the family didn't let their guard down completely. They checked on each other frequently, and the girls now slept two to a bed.

But their adversary, having grown strong from feeding off the family's fear, would wait no longer.

On a Sunday morning at 3:00 a.m., Lisa and Katie woke up to the sound of loud, crashing footsteps coming right toward their door. To their tremendous relief, the footsteps passed by their door and continued down the hall. Then they stopped. Right in front of Aubrey and Ellie's room. Aubrey was already awake. She too had awoken at 3:00 a.m., drenched in sweat and terrified of something as yet unseen. She shook her cousin awake. "It's at our door!" she shouted. The two girls watched in horror as their door swung open and a large black mass slithered into the room. The thing jumped on the girls' waterbed with such force that they were tossed around like a rowboat in a storm. Aubrey then felt the thing's crushing weight push down on her chest, making it hard for her to breathe. Ellie screamed for Judy, who later recounted how simply running across the hall took every fiber of her being. She felt like she was running in slow motion, her legs like leaden posts. When she finally reached the room, which was as cold as a refrigerator, Judy launched herself onto the bed and covered the girls with her own body. Out of the corner of her eye, she saw something dark race through the door.

A moment later, screams emanated from Lisa and Katie's room. This time it was not a shapeless mass that materialized, but a hairy beast, and it stood at the foot of the girls' bed. They pulled the covers over their heads and then Lisa felt it crawl on top of her. As she lay frozen in fear and unable to speak or move, the beast roared and in a deep male voice spewed forth a litany of sadistic and obscene things it was going to do to her. Lisa thought she was going to die. Just then, Judy burst through the doorway in a rage, not knowing or caring what was there but ready to fight for her kids. Luckily, she didn't have to; the beast dissolved into a black blur and faded away through the window. Though she hated to do it, Judy gathered everyone together and drove to her mother's house. Thankfully, the family was spared any further torments that night. The next morning, fearing for her mother's safety if she stayed too long, Judy reluctantly brought the girls back home.

For a blessed but short time after this 3:00 a.m. rampage, there were no physical attacks on the McGraths. The two oldest girls, however, found themselves battling a new type of assault, a psychological one that left them questioning their mental health. Ellie was affected the most. When she was cooking, she would get overwhelming urges to grab a knife and stab someone. She found herself fantasizing about hurting other family members. Often she found herself fantasizing about hurting herself. Aubrey battled an obsession with her hands. They moved on their own, she recalled, in directions and gestures against her will. Most horrifically was when she envisioned her hands turning into claws. Claws she wanted to scratch and rip people apart with. Aubrey described those times as feeling like she was splitting into two sides, a good and a bad. As they would be told later, they were experiencing classic signs of demonic oppression, wherein the evil entity amplifies a person's fear, anger, hatred, and other negative emotions and uses them to sow doubt in the victim's mind as to their self-worth and sanity.

Having thus set the stage, the demon wasted no time in attacking again. It was midnight a few weeks later when Katie and Lisa awoke to the harrowing sense of a malevolent presence close by. Lisa feigned sleep, but Katie stole a look toward the door and saw standing there a tall shadow figure. It suddenly rushed to the end of the bed and then, in an instant, it was on top of her. It smothered Katie with its weight, its formless mass seeping into every fold of her body. Katie struggled to move and to breathe as the thing pressed so hard on her she thought it would push her right through the bed. After what seemed an eternity, she felt her lungs release and she yelled out. Lisa tried to help her sister by swatting the bed with her pillow and shouting, "Go away!" Moments later, Judy arrived, wrapping the girls in her arms until Katie could finally talk and tell them *it* had left.

But not for long. Its lustful desire to terrorize and hurt the McGrath females had just begun. A few weeks later, Ellie was awakened by a thunderous noise, as if someone was banging on the walls with a sledgehammer. Remarkably, no one else in the house heard anything, not even her sleeping companion, Aubrey. As Ellie strained to see in the semi-darkness of her room, she made out the shadowy figure of a man staring at her from the end of the bed. She immediately knew that whatever it was, it was evil and wanted to hurt or kill her. She tried to wake Aubrey but the entity was on top of her before she could speak or move. As it did with Katie, it smothered Ellie with its weight, but this time it entered its victim's body in a painful sexual manner. As horrible as the physical rape was, the mental assault was worse. It invaded her mind with foul and evil thoughts, "sickening beyond belief," as Ellie described them. While the physical act only lasted a few moments, the visions in Ellie's mind haunted her for years afterward.

Though she escaped from harm the night of Ellie's assault, Aubrey would soon become the demon's third victim about two months later. She had the room to herself, as Ellie had fallen asleep downstairs on the couch watching television. She recalled having a restless night before finally deciding to get up for a glass of milk and rousing Ellie. She stood at the edge of the bed looking for her slippers when she saw what appeared to be a man sitting in her chair. But there was something not quite right about him. He was dark and featureless, and his shape kept changing and shimmering like a faulty hologram. He chuckled menacingly and started staggering toward Aubrey, who was now transfixed by the sudden change in her surroundings. Her whole room had become distorted and wavy, matching the manner of the figure walking toward her. She felt disoriented and about to fall when the "man" pushed her down on the bed. Though in her mind she was flailing and fighting, she was, in reality, helpless beneath the entity's weight. She couldn't see it, but she could smell its rancid odor and could feel it moving along her legs and back, pushing her body hard into the mattress and her face into the pillow. It sodomized her, and then left her alone and weeping and ashamed.

Judy had had enough. If the local churches didn't want to help her family, she would find someone who would. She reached out to a television documentary series that reported on real-life cases of the paranormal, UFOs, cryptid creatures, and other unexplained phenomena. The show profiled the McGraths on one of its 30-minute episodes but couldn't offer any immediate assistance beyond that. Judy hoped someone would see their plight who could help. A few months later, her prayers were answered. A producer on the show reached out to the well-known paranormal experts Ed and Lorraine Warren and asked if they could look into the case. The producer wanted to do a follow-up episode on the family that included the findings of professional investigators. The Warrens agreed and in turn reached out to a colleague, New York City police officer Ralph Sarchie, to assist them. Sarchie, who had been mentored in demonology and exorcism by the Warrens and Jesuit writer Father Malachi Martin of *Hostage to the Devil* fame, had seen the documentary and knew the McGraths were dealing with a particularly nasty demon whose ultimate goal was the possession and/or death of the family members.

The Warrens and Sarchie met with the McGraths on a stormy afternoon in early spring. While Ed and Lorraine interviewed each of the family members, Ralph walked through the house to get an initial impression. When he entered the basement, a strong sense of dread overcame him and made him stop in his tracks. He later learned that this was the part of the house used by Gilliam and his satanic cohorts for their heinous rituals. He quickly left and went back upstairs. As he made his way toward the kitchen, something caught his eye. Gliding past the glass double doors that led from the dining room to the patio was a formless black mass. Ralph had seen such manifestations before in his work, and after watching it pass through the outside wall, he followed it out to the patio, where, of course, there was nothing to be seen.

Ralph rejoined the others and listened to the incredulous accounts of the horrors everyone had experienced over the last several years. Judy ended the interview with her own account of a solitary nocturnal assault. She had kept the incident to herself up to now, but hearing her daughters and niece courageously come forth with their horrific and deeply personal testimonies, she felt compelled to do the same. It happened one evening when she was unusually tired and went to bed early. She was in the early stages of sleep when she was awakened by a presence inside her room. As she focused her eyes, she couldn't believe what she was seeing. A huge, hairy monster was staring at her. It stood upright like a man but had the longest arms Judy had ever seen. Instead of fingers, its huge hands ended in menacingly-looking claws. *It's a beast!* Judy thought to herself. She screamed at it: "Get away from me!" But the thing was soon upon her, smothering her body with its own. A thunderous roar filled the room and sent vibrations up and down Judy's spine. Then she felt the beast enter her. The pain was so excruciating she expected — indeed, hoped — to pass out. Thankfully, the assault ended quickly, and as mysteriously as it had appeared, the beast vanished.

The Warrens and Ralph explained to the forlorn family that they were dealing with an incubus, a markedly vile demon that sexually terrorizes its victims. Although demons have no gender, they can take on either a male or female form in order to violate their victims. If the demon is in the form of a man, it's called an incubus. A female version is called a succubus. While they get no pleasure in the sexual acts themselves, they thrive on the terror, humiliation, and degradation they instill in their prey. Legends and lore about these demons go back to ancient days, the earliest known written reference having been recorded in Mesopotamia around 2400 BC. The Christian theologians Augustine and Aquinas wrote about them, as did King James in his work *Daemonologie*. They have appeared in all cultures and among all creeds. Often they present themselves as stunningly attractive when they begin the seduction of their victims. But at other times, as in the case of the McGraths, they seek simply to overwhelm with violence and terror, manifesting as the nightmarish creatures that they are. Given the perverse nature of the crimes committed previously in the house—the molestation of children—it was little surprise that a wanton, rampaging demon of lust was attracted to the scene. Now it was time to end its reign of terror and banish it for good.

Ed and Lorraine gathered all the family members in one room and stayed with them while Ralph performed an exorcism on the house. Going room to room, Ralph burned blessed incense and showered holy water on everything he could. Then, while tightly grasping a relic of the True Cross in his hand, he recited the ritual prayers of the Church, his eyes and other senses on high alert for demonic activity. Ralph has never been shy about expressing his religious beliefs, which are grounded in traditional Roman Catholicism. He believes faith, virtue, and grace are necessary for success in what he terms "the Work," investigating cases of demonic possession and oppression, as well as assisting with and performing exorcisms. These beliefs carried him through the next several hours, when finally around midnight—ten hours after first setting foot in the McGrath house—he closed his prayer book and took note of the silence. He was somewhat surprised the demon didn't manifest itself in some manner during the ritual, but also thankful to be spared those theatrics. His only scare came when the refrigerator turned on unexpectedly with a loud *click* while he was standing in the kitchen doorway. As he recalled, he aged about ten years in that one second. Though there had been no signs of the demon, only time would tell if the exorcism was effective.

It was a year later when Judy called Ed Warren to happily report that there had been no more trouble since the exorcism. Often in similar situations, the demon either goes dormant or leaves and comes back. Neither seemed to be the case here. In his account of the story, Ralph wrote that the psychological fortitude of the family played an important role in their survival. Instead of allowing the demon to break them apart, they banded together during the worst times. By sharing their fears and emotions, they avoided the demon's attempts to drive them to isolation and despair.

Unfortunately, there is an endless pool of debauchery and depravity in the world that attracts such demons like sharks to blood. And while most of the time, the attack is on the one who "asked for it," attacks still come to the unsuspecting and innocent. The McGraths were fortunate. They escaped the clutches of a horrific predator. Many, unfortunately, are still grappling with theirs.

Attack of the Elementals

For Manny and Corina Ocampo, the opportunity to build their dream home from scratch was a fairy tale come true. The young Filipino couple had recently bought Corina's uncle's old house after he relocated his family to the United States. The property, located on the outskirts of the City of Valenzuela, offered a reasonable commute to the couple's jobs while providing indoor space and outdoor greenery that their crowded downtown condo sorely lacked. Having three energetic young children, the Ocampos were confident their decision was the right one. The only drawback was the house itself: it required major repairs and updating. Financially, the renovations weren't a problem, but the Ocampos decided that if they were going to go to that much trouble, they may as well go a step further and raze the old house completely. That way they could plan and construct a new home that would be perfectly fitted for their family.

After nine long months of patiently dealing with the pleasures and pains of new house construction, the Ocampos finally moved in. They were not disappointed. For the whole first year, the family lived in carefree bliss in their new spacious dwelling. There was plenty of room for the children to play, there were modern amenities for all to enjoy, and the work commute for Manny and Corina, while not perfect, was still better than their old one. The Ocampos were also fortunate in that they could employ two live-in *yayas* (care providers) for their children. These young ladies were not only essential to keeping the household running smoothly, but they were as much a part of the Ocampo family as any birthright member. Which is why after that first year, when the *yayas* reported strange occurrences, Manny and Corina listened.

The trouble began when the *yayas* started hearing odd noises around noon in their upstairs bedroom. It sounded as if someone was throwing pebbles through the window, which was usually open to catch much-desired tropical breezes. Yet when the girls investigated, even to the point of crawling around and looking under furniture, there were never any foreign objects to be seen. Making the noises even stranger was the fact that it simply wasn't possible to throw anything through the window because a large yucca tree stood between the street and the house. It was possible, of course, that a person could have climbed the tree and tossed something in, but no one was ever discovered in or even around the tree when the "pebbles" were heard hitting the window frames and floors.

Invisible projectiles were bad enough, but the disturbances soon became more personal. One night when one of the *yayas* woke up to use the bathroom, she felt the eerie sensation of being followed down the hall. Repeated glances over her shoulder showed no one behind her, but she couldn't shake the feeling. She felt somewhat better when she entered the bathroom and closed the door, but she had no sooner sat down on the toilet when the door burst open and a cold wind blew through the room, sending a plastic tumbler and some hair accessories flying across the vanity.

Manny also felt that same sensation of being watched on several occasions. The Ocampos had an outdoor kitchen that they used often for entertaining or for family meals when the weather was nice. Manny often watched television out there late at night so he could have the volume up and not disturb anyone. While the television had always worked fine in the past, it began having frequent technical problems around the same time the yayas were experiencing their odd events. In frustration, Manny would often end his late-night viewing early and set about going to bed. As he came inside, though, he couldn't help but feel that "something" was coming in behind him. He shook off the feeling as best he could, but he remained on edge as the strange sensation followed him up the stairs to the bedroom.

Around this same time, Corina was busy with her own mysterious dealings, although in a much different way. A journalist by trade, Corina had recently volunteered to cover "the Halloween beat," writing articles about paranormal subjects and specifically about priests who served as exorcists. Differentiating fact from fiction and presenting exorcists in a more positive light was, to Corina, not only a journalistic challenge but also a way to serve in her church. Little did she know at the time she took on the assignment that she would soon be chronicling her own family's story.

Corina knew, of course, about the strange noises in the upstairs bedroom and the unnerving sensation of being watched that some of the household members reported. But one morning, the *yayas* came to her with a new and disturbing—and very visible—oddity. On the back of both girls' legs there had grown, overnight, hard lumps just beneath the skin. They went to the community health center immediately but came back home with no answers. Corina then sent them to her doctor, and again they came back with no viable explanation. The lumps were probably just benign cysts, they were told, that would eventually subside on their own.

By now, having dealt with a number of unexplainable phenomena, the Ocampo family suspected they were dealing with something supernatural. Corina brought the subject up to her parish priest, Father Jerome, the next time she met with him for an article interview. Father Jerome was himself involved in the deliverance ministry and was often called on for help by parishioners who believed they had an "extraordinary" problem in their home. In addition to being a fount of knowledge, it was rumored that Father Jerome was also a psychic "sensitive," someone who could detect the presence of unseen spirits. The priest agreed to meet with the girls and arrived at the Ocampo house the next day. After asking some questions of the *yayas* and other family members about their strange experiences, Father Jerome prayed over the girls and then went through the house, inspecting and blessing it room by room. Whether by prayer or natural doing, the lumps on the girls' legs vanished a few days later.

Before he left, Father Jerome told Corina that he believed the family was dealing with either a *kapre* or a *tikbalang*, Filipino names for elemental spirits (spirits who reside in nature), and that their particular elemental tormentor lived in the yucca tree overlooking their second-story window. He promised to offer prayers to banish the spirit, and then instructed Corina to do something special that would help in getting rid of it. He wanted her to burn a vinyl record under the yucca. The elemental wouldn't be able to stand the awful smell and would likely leave. Corina looked at the priest as if he had lost his mind, all the while knowing that she was desperate enough to try it. The next day, her only decision was choosing between classical and pop.

* * *

Fairies, pixies, nymphs, gnomes, elves, leprechauns, sprites, brownies, trolls—these and many other names have been given throughout history and in many different cultures to a group of non-human entities collectively cataloged as "elementals." In the Philippines, they are called lamang lupa, engkanto, kapre and tikbalang, among other names. Elemental spirits are also known as "nature spirits" and are said to occupy and influence the major "elements" of nature, namely earth, water, fire, and air. For example, according to lore, gnomes are earth elementals because they prefer to live in caves and deep forests where they exercise power over rocks, minerals, flowers, and trees. Fairies are air elementals that cleanse the air with winds, help birds in their migrations, and oversee the pollination of flowers.

The basis for belief in elemental spirits dates back to the ancient Greeks, who called all otherworldly beings *daemons*, including their lesser gods, muses, guardian spirits, spirits of place, and spirits of the four elements. In the 16th century, Swiss physician and philosopher Paracelsus formalized the classification of the nature spirits in his treatise, *A Book on Nymphs, Sylphs, Pygmies, and Salamanders, and on the Other Spirits*. He wrote the book, he said, to "describe the creatures that are outside the cognizance of the light of nature." Interestingly, Paracelsus did not consider these beings to be pure spirits, but as something between a spirit and a creature. He further described them as generally invisible to humans, but as also having physical and humanoid bodies, as well as other human-like behaviors such as sleeping, eating, and wearing clothes. Unlike humans, they are able to move through their own elements (rocks, for example) as easily as we walk through air. And, of course, they have powers and abilities outside the human realm that to humans would seem magical.

It is these seemingly miraculous powers that have inspired humans throughout the ages to revere and even worship these creatures. Paracelsus himself was so enchanted by elementals that he referred to them as "divine objects" and proclaimed he was in bliss when describing them. In modern times, elementals continue to be revered and invoked by followers of nature-based religions, as well as groups that continue ancient pagan customs such as Druids, and newer groups like Wiccans.

Elementals may have been painted in a captivating and fantastic light by philosophers and folklorists through the centuries, but there has been, and remains, much disagreement as to not only their very existence but also their nature. As previously mentioned, the ancient Greeks used the word *daemon* for those preternatural beings that existed between the realms of the gods and mankind. With the rise of Judeo-Christian traditions, that word and everything it represented became the more familiar word "demon." The elementals did not escape this new classification. Athanasius of Alexandria, an early Church Father of the 4th century, talked of "demons" that occupied springs, rivers, trees, and stones, and who "cheated men by deceptive appearances."

Carrying on that warning in our times are exorcists like Father Jose Francisco Syquia, director of the Archdiocese of Manila's office of exorcism, who unequivocally states that these spirits are all really demons in disguise and should not be encouraged, revered, or interacted with in any way. "Never say *tabi-tabi-po*," he exhorts, in reference to the Filipino tradition of politely asking any spirits present to "excuse you" when entering someone's home or other location. "You're submitting yourself to fallen angels," the priest warns. He also warns that there are no "white" and "black" elementals, some that bring good luck and some that bring bad. They are all evil, and any offer of good fortune, health, or prosperity will always result in the demon demanding payback, the ultimate, of course, being one's soul. He further adds:

"There is no such thing as mutual peaceful coexistence with elementals or nature spirits since no one in his right mind would want an invisible liar and murderer filled with hatred in one's home. They will always clandestinely affect the persons in the home in a negative manner…through sicknesses like heart attacks, headaches, and stomach aches; relational problems and division within the family; emotional and psychological illnesses like impatience, anger, and depression; temptations like lust, pride, and sloth in one's prayer life; weakening faith and even failures in businesses."

* * *

While the Ocampo family had experienced some supernatural harassment, the disturbances had not yet reached exorcism level, and Corina was determined to keep it that way. So the morning after Father Jerome's house visit, she dutifully brought her copy of Journey's *Escape* album out to the base of the yucca tree and set the record on fire. As she watched wisps of putrid-smelling smoke swirl upwards, she wondered how it came to be that a spiteful spirit was living in a tree by her house and targeting her family with its malicious mayhem. Perhaps the smell will drive it away like Father Jerome said, Corina hoped silently. Unable to stand the odor any longer herself, she went back inside and shut the door and windows.

A few days later, the Ocampos left for a long-awaited vacation to Hong Kong, happily leaving the yucca and its resident imp far behind. Or so they thought. Looking back on the trip, Corina clearly sees the connection. It turned out that Father Jerome was right: the elemental didn't like the smell of the burning record. But instead of leaving, it decided to take its displeasure out on the person responsible.

The trouble started when Corina developed a fever on the plane. By the time the family reached their hotel, she was also experiencing stomach cramps and waved off having dinner out. After Manny, the yayas, and the kids left to eat, Corina pulled the curtains closed and settled under the bed covers. Five minutes later, she was in the bathroom losing everything she had eaten earlier in the day. Waves of dizziness, cramping, and vomiting kept her racing between the bed and bath. After her final bout in the bathroom, she glanced in the mirror expecting to see a bedraggled version of herself but instead saw a woman she didn't recognize. Corina peered closer at the image, wondering if her illness had made her delusional. Maybe it was her, but then she wondered, why was that woman's mouth closed when hers was open to breathe easier? Just then, the other woman's face began to contort freakishly and a twisted, perverse smile appeared on her lips. Terrified, Corina ran out of the bathroom and jumped under her bed covers. Shock, exhaustion, and lingering dizziness took control and she soon passed out.

Corina recovered quickly enough to enjoy the rest of the vacation with her family. But unfortunately, more trouble ensued after coming back home. Personal possessions like jewelry and wallets went missing, only to reappear in the most unlikely of places, such as in a potted plant or on the floor of the shed that hadn't been unlocked for weeks. Lights and appliances randomly went on and off by themselves, the most shocking example happening when Manny and Corina were drinking tea in the kitchen one night and suddenly one of the gas burners on the stove whooshed alive with an energetic flame. The sound of pebbles being thrown through the yayas' upstairs window continued as well. One afternoon when it occurred, the girls went to investigate and were astounded to see, not rocks on the floor, but glass from their shattered wall mirror.

Driven by the need for some answers, Corina used her journalism skills to dig a little deeper into her family's past. She found out that before she and Manny bought their property from her uncle, he had rented it for a few years to another relative, Corina's uncle-in-law, Carlos. Carlos had a business that he decided could use a little boost, so he invoked the aid of a *duwende*, an elf-like elemental believed to bring about good luck. Witnesses who knew Carlos said that he catered to the *duwende* by leaving out bits of food and even building a tiny house for it and any roaming elementals to use.

Although Carlos's business thrived while he resided in this home, eventually he needed to move his family to a new location. According to stories Corina unearthed, his elemental friends moved with him. But now instead of bringing luck and good fortune, the spirits occupied themselves by frightening and harassing Carlos's children and grandchildren in their new house. One cousin of Corina's reported seeing a luminous green man standing in the hallway one night. Another said she saw a strange woman with long, filthy hair who wouldn't answer when spoken to and who disappeared in the flick of an eye. And then there were the accounts of "small people" who poked the children from under their pillows and bed covers as they tried to sleep.

The predicament the Ocampos were in now made more sense to Corina. From talking with Father Jerome and Father Syquia, she knew that it was common for wily spirits to offer promises of prosperity, protection, or "good luck" to win a family's trust and gain access to their home and their members. Soon after, their true natures and malevolent desires always came to light. The priests also told Corina it was likely that the spirit (or spirits) attacking her family had always lived on that property, residing in old trees, shrubs, mounds of dirt, and the like, and had become displaced with the construction of their new house. Not only were they forced to move, say to the yucca tree, but they were also angered and riled up by the disturbance.

Corina couldn't help but wonder just how many elementals were at one time living on the property. It appeared that some had left with Carlos, but obviously some had stayed behind. She was reminded of this in a terrifying way one night when she awoke at 3:00 a.m. to the sound of screeching metal. She roused Manny awake, and the two of them watched in amazement as the bulb in their night lamp slowly turned by itself in its socket, then popped out of the lamp and flew across the room still aglow. It landed, remarkably, without breaking near the crib of their baby.

Corina and Manny were now more than ever concerned for the safety of their children. They reached out to their priest friends, asking for more prayers and another blessing of their house. For days after, though she had been assured by Father Jerome that the spirits had now been banished after the latest deliverance session, Corina experienced constant anxiety as the light bulb incident played repeatedly in her mind. Thankful for Father Jerome's help, and in no way critical of his efforts, she nonetheless craved a different kind of reassurance. One that came from God Himself. And so, in prayer one day, she asked God for a sign.

Later that afternoon, Corina took her children to their ice skating lessons. While waiting for them, she walked around, browsing the windows of the little shops in the area before coming upon a church. She stepped inside and joined the celebration of a Mass that had just started. She prayed for the protection of her family and once again asked God for a sign that everything would be all right. Afterward, while walking back to the skating rink, she noticed a queue of empty taxis slowly passing by her. She smiled as she read the sign on the first one: "San Gabriel." God's messenger. The second taxi in line had another eye-catching sign on it: "*Ina ng Awa,*" a reference to Mary, the Queen of Angels and the saint demons are most afraid of. And then a third taxi rolled forward, this one inscribed with the words *Santo Christo*.

Corina felt her anxiety immediately lift. She had asked for a sign and received three. She went home with her children knowing their home was no longer troubled by evil spirits. And from that day forward, it never was.

The Devil in Los Angeles

The following two stories come from the collected experiences of retired L.A. County Sheriff's Deputy Jesse Romero. During his stint with the LASD, Jesse came into contact with strange people and terrifying events on a regular basis. Most cases could be explained by human reason. Many could not. Because Jesse was (and still is) an active member of his church, serving as an apologist, an evangelist, and a deliverance expert, he was able to recognize when there was a supernatural element to his encounters. He tells about many of these experiences in his book *The Devil in the City of Angels: My Encounters With the Diabolical.*

Dancing With the Devil

Serena braced herself against the wave of nausea churning in her stomach. She knew she should have eaten something before the show, just a slice of bread even. Anything to soak up the acid that seemed to continually plague her digestive tract the past few months. Despite her discomfort, Serena kicked her legs higher, catching the pole above her head while arching her head back in seductive playfulness, a move she knew would always elicit bawdy cheers from her audience.

Serena was a favorite at the "gentleman's club." She was an alluring, athletic dancer who knew how to work a male crowd. But what started out as fun in the beginning of her employment was now becoming stranger . . . and scarier.

There were always the unsavory characters who tried to take her home, slip her drugs, or even, on a few occasions, assault her, though it never got too extreme before club security stepped in. But what had been happening lately was something not even the beefiest bouncer could do anything about. Now when Serena performed her routine on stage, the men in the audience appeared to transform. Their faces changed before her eyes into diabolical visages, some with classic demonic features of red eyes and horns, others with more human but grotesquely deformed looks.

When it first started happening, Serena assumed it was the drugs. She had started taking them from day one at the club; it was the only way she could get up on stage and dance naked. But when she began seeing the demonic faces, she quit cold turkey. She had enough experience and confidence by now that she could do her show sober. Yet she continued to see the horrible faces and feel the lustful, hateful intentions they projected at her. It was why her stomach was so upset now when she took the stage.

Two more nights, she told herself. *Just get through two more nights*. Serena had already informed her manager she was quitting at the end of the week. Not only couldn't she handle seeing the frightening visions, but getting off drugs had given her a newfound clarity about the direction she wanted her life to go in. And it wasn't back on the stripper's stage.

She grasped the pole tighter and steeled herself for the final moves that would end one more hellish night. As she righted herself and was about to spin down, she stopped abruptly. Looking out into the audience, she saw the familiar fiendish faces, but this time she saw something new: instead of shoes at the bottom of the men's pants, she saw goat hooves. She jumped down from the pole and ran off the stage, nearly forgetting to put on her clothes before she raced out the back door for the last time.

* * *

Serena's intentions to live a better life got off to a rocky start. She may have quit the stripper's job, but the addictive pull of drugs and alcohol was too much for her to overcome completely. She floundered for several years, going in and out of rehab, and jumping from job to job to make ends meet. Her new boyfriend was a married man, and any suggestion from a family member or friend that what she was doing was wrong was met with stern defiance and salty language. Serena also became involved with the occult, going so far as employing witches to put curses on her enemies.

After eventually ending the relationship with her boyfriend, Serena slowly started to make other changes in her life. She finally kicked her drug and alcohol habits, found a steady job, and began attending church again. She had been raised Catholic and was feeling more and more a desire to return to her faith. While her loved ones were thrilled with her new lifestyle changes, other unseen actors in her life were decidedly not.

Serena's involvement in the occult had attracted, as it always does, the attention of unwelcome, evil spirits. She was likely more vulnerable by the added factors of her past substance abuse and immoral lifestyle choices. Whatever the root cause, these entities attached themselves to her while she remained completely unaware. But when she threatened their existence by taking a renewed interest in God and the Church, their hatred and evil intent could remain hidden no more.

* * *

Her apartment door may have been locked, but Serena felt far from safe. She couldn't shake the feeling that something she couldn't see was watching her. Something dark and threatening. She had been feeling this way for a while now and wondered if she was going crazy. Hardly a day passed that she didn't see shadows dart across her peripheral vision and voices whispering in her ear when she was alone. Her lights flickered all the time, even after she changed bulbs. And getting a good night's sleep was a luxury, given the frequent rapping noises in her walls after midnight.

Not caring if she came across as a loon, Serena finally confided in a neighbor. This same woman had been instrumental in getting Serena to come back to church, so when she heard about the strange activity in Serena's apartment, she suspected that something foul was afoot. She invited Serena to a presentation on spiritual warfare that was being given by Jesse Romero, a Catholic lay evangelist and deliverance expert. Serena agreed and accompanied her neighbor to the event the next evening.

As she sat there in the packed church hall, Serena felt increasingly uncomfortable. The ominous presence that had been distressing her at home was not only with her now but was growing in strength and maliciousness. The more Jesse talked, the more this *thing* squirmed its way into Serena's thoughts and actions. She started having difficulty controlling her facial expressions and she began making inappropriate noises during the presentation. Soon her voice grew louder and louder, the entity firmly entrenched within her and raging against the talk about God and grace and the casting out of demons.

"Jesse, Jesse, help me! It's burning! Get him out, get him out!" Serena's shouts turned the crowd's heads toward her, and then, to the dismay of all watching, she slithered out of her chair and down to the floor like a snake. Her eyes turned pitch black as she writhed around in a demonic trance. Many of the attendees were so frightened at the spectacle that they fled the building. Those that stayed began praying in earnest as Jesse cautiously approached the besieged woman.

"Help me! It burns! Get him out of my stomach. Get him out!"

Jesse, his wife, and another man named Eddie surrounded Serena and soon couldn't believe what they were seeing.

"We saw her stomach rising up and then going back down like 'whack-a-moles' at a carnival," Jesse said. "Her stomach would rise in different areas and then go back down. It reminded me of the movie *Alien* where this space alien came out of the protagonist's stomach."

They managed to carry Serena out to the back patio to keep her out of sight of the remaining attendees, many of whom were visibly shaken at the sights and sounds before them. Jesse dashed over to the church sacristy to get his pastor, but the priest was just about to start Mass. He gave Jesse his blessing and told him, "You know what to do."

Enlisting the help of two more able-bodied parishioners, Jesse and his assistants prayed over Serena using the prayers of the *Auxilium Christianorum*, an organization founded by two exorcists that draws its power to battle the demonic from the united daily prayer of its tens of thousands of members. As the group prayed, the demon continued to manifest, twisting and contorting Serena's body in cruel, mocking ways, and making her stomach continue to rise and fall like something was trying to get out. Finally, after forty minutes of intense ministration, the convulsions stopped and Serena lay still. After another few minutes, she opened her eyes, which to everyone's relief were clear and normal-looking. Tears started to run down her face as she softly said, "It left. Thank you, thank you. It left."

The demon really did leave Serena. She returned to the full practice of her faith and was not further troubled by diabolic entities. She knows she can't change her past, but she has learned from it. And she will tell all who are willing to listen to not put themselves in situations that might attract unwanted attention from evildoers, whether they be from this realm or another.

Sacrificed to Satan

Natalia's childhood was the very definition of a nightmare. Her father was a leader in a southern California branch of the satanic cult La Santa Muerte. When Natalia was very young, her father consecrated her to the devil in a black magic ritual. Throughout her childhood and into her older teen years, she was forced to participate in animal and human sacrifices, sexual orgies, drinking animal and human blood, grave desecration, vandalizing sacred places, casting curses and spells, and stealing consecrated communion wafers from Catholic churches. If Natalia resisted doing any of these things, members of the cult would beat and torture her.

Once a year, Natalia was taken to a week-long "discipleship" camp in the middle of the desert, where a high satanic priest gave lectures and demonstrations in the finer points of the dark arts. One night while the attendees were gathered around a campfire, the priest changed into a large black wolf before their very eyes. In his new embodiment, he circled the terrified onlookers in a predatory manner, instilling fear and asserting his authority. Then he transformed back into a man and continued his occult oration, leaving the stunned disciples in a bizarre state of shock and awe.

When she was eighteen, Natalia and her mother—who wasn't a member of the cult and who had struggled to practice Catholicism in secret to not upset her husband—left Natalia's father for good and moved to Mexico. There Natalia took up the practice of her mother's faith, while her father, in the interim, committed suicide.

While Natalia may have left the satanic sect in theory, in reality the sect did not leave her. Having been exposed to so much evil over her young life, and having been "given" to the very Prince of Evil in a satanic ritual, Natalia could not escape the long-reaching tentacles of the demons her father had sicced on her. On a near-daily basis, she endured vexation and torment from unseen forces until finally, fearing for her sanity as well as her life, she sought the help of the Church. Diocesan exorcists in Guadalajara and Mexico City examined her carefully and determined that Natalia exhibited all of the signs of demonic possession:

1. A sudden ability to speak and understand an unknown language;
2. The ability to divulge future and hidden events;
3. Abnormal physical strength;
4. The detection of the holy and a vehement aversion to it.

And so began almost a decade of exorcisms. From age 19 to 29, Natalia underwent multiple exorcisms in Mexico. She kept a journal of each one and of the progress she felt was being made. But unfortunately, members of her father's cult found out where she was living and began harassing her and her mother, forcing them to move back to the United States. For a short while, Natalia's life in Los Angeles was pleasantly uneventful, so much so that she let her religious practices lapse and bounced around from church to church without a firm commitment to any.

With her guard down, the enemy came back, and Natalia began experiencing the same demonic oppression she had in Mexico. During this period of persecution — as if attacks from the supernatural realm weren't enough — Natalia's apartment was burglarized. The responding officer was L.A. County Sheriff's Deputy Jesse Romero, who happened to also be a lay Catholic evangelist. While giving her burglary statement to Jesse, an emotionally distraught Natalia also opened up about her spiritual battle. Jesse advised her to seek the help of local priest Father Stephanos, who was renowned for his work in the areas of healing and spiritual warfare.

Natalia took Jesse's advice and underwent a series of prayer and deliverance sessions with Father Stephanos while also becoming a permanent member of the parish and renewing her faith traditions. About a year later, Father Stephanos reached out to Jesse and asked if he would participate in a special deliverance session for Natalia that was to be held later in the week. Jesse had made such a positive impression on Natalia when she first met him that the priest thought his presence would be helpful.

The deliverance date arrived, and gathered at the church with Father Stephanos were Natalia, her mother, three brothers, and Jesse and his wife. When Jesse looked curiously at an exercise mat one of the brothers brought along, he was told it was needed to minimize injuries. When the demon manifested, the brother explained, it took over Natalia's body and caused her to violently thrash around with inhuman strength. Jesse silently hoped that wouldn't happen this night, but nonetheless braced himself as Father Stephanos settled Natalia in a chair about fifteen feet from the main altar.

The priest began with a prayer for protection for all of those assisting, and then he held before Natalia a consecrated communion wafer, what Catholics believe to be the Body of Christ. At this, Jesse reported in his book *The Devil in the City of Angels*, the demon manifested:

"Her body expanded like a pufferfish [and] her arms and legs became as hard as wood...She began speaking in different languages. It sounded like gibberish. She pointed to one of her brothers and disclosed some hidden and embarrassing unconfessed sins about her brother's lifestyle. This brother was so humiliated that he just stood there petrified and did not help in prayer or in holding her down."

As in the past, this night also saw Natalia respond with frightening violence to those who ministered around her. Her eyes turned pitch black like pieces of coal and her face twisted up in rage. She began throwing punches like a boxer, connecting one of them squarely with Father Stephanos's jaw. She clawed at the necks and hands of those wearing crosses or holding rosaries. She grunted like a pig and growled like a dog. When splashed with holy water, she howled as if the very fires of hell were burning her. Repeated attempts to constrain her were futile, and during one such struggle she broke free, grabbed Jesse by the front of his shirt, and threw him against the wall like he weighed no more than a sack of potatoes.

His ego bruised more than his body, Jesse jumped back up and assisted Natalia's mother and brothers in holding Natalia down on her stomach. Jesse remembered her arms being as hard as wood planks, and how on her right arm that he was trying to hold steady, three scratches suddenly materialized before his eyes and began to bleed. Then Natalia started to make strange signals with her fingers while muttering in unfamiliar gibberish. Father Stephanos warned that she was summoning demons; no sooner had he said this than loud, unnerving pounding reverberated from every door in the church. The priest immediately doused Natalia's hands with holy water and the pounding stopped.

Father Stephanos then took out his *Manual of Minor Exorcisms* along with his Bible and began reciting the ancient prayers and scriptures that have been used for casting out demons for centuries. For three hours, the group struggled to keep Natalia subdued while Father Stephanos prayed over her. Seeing little positive effect thus far, the priest instructed everyone there to join him in praying to Mary. As they recited the Hail Mary in English and Spanish, Natalia reacted with renewed vigor. She writhed and strained against her handlers and screamed as if being tortured. "It sounded like we dropped a microphone into hell," Jesse recalled. But it was when Father Stephanos switched to saying the prayer in Latin that the demon protested the most vehemently.

"Ave Maria, gratia plena, Dominus tecum ..."

"Get her off me! Get her off me!" Natalia screamed in a guttural voice not her own.

"Who?" demanded Father Stephanos.

"The woman, the woman, get her off me!"

With revived strength and hope, the group joined Father Stephanos in reciting the Latin prayer. They knew they were close to vanquishing Natalia's demon, but it wouldn't leave without one final and shocking manifestation.

"She kept yelling (the voice was not hers) as if she were in excruciating pain," reported Jesse, "and then went flat on her stomach in a cruciform position. Her body began getting long as if something was on top of her and smashing her like a pancake. I rubbed both of my eyes with my fist and made sure that I was not hallucinating, but my wife verified that she saw the same thing on the drive home."

Finally, the gruesome physical contortions stopped and Natalia's body went back to normal like an accordion relaxing back into its original shape. A transcendental quiet descended upon the group, and after several minutes Father Stephanos announced that the demon had left. Natalia's mother and brothers helped her up. She was exhausted but at peace, and in an encouraging sign that she was indeed demon-free, she asked the priest if she could receive Holy Communion.

* * *

Natalia's story highlights some important concepts in the lore of demonic possession and exorcism. One is that is not uncommon for exorcisms to take longer than one session. Depending on the strength of the demon(s), how many are present, their origin of entry, and the faith and/or behavior of the victim, successful exorcisms can take days, months, sometimes even years to complete.

Natalia also had the most unfortunate circumstance of being cursed by her father when he "sacrificed" her to Satan as a child. The former chief exorcist of Rome, now deceased, Father Gabriele Amorth spoke often on the subject of curses, as they are extremely common not only in Italy but all over the world. He wrote: "Curses invoke evil, and the origin of all evil is demonic. When curses are spoken with true perfidy, especially if there is a blood relationship between the one who casts them and the accursed, the outcome can be terrible."

Natalia did indeed suffer terrible consequences from her father's evil acts, and her story should be a warning to us all of the power of demonic forces. But it should also, more importantly, give us hope that there is no evil deed that can't be undone, for the Light will always drive out the dark.

Doris Bither's Poltergeist

Doris Bither and her four children had just moved into the small house on Braddock Drive in Culver City, California, and not knowing anyone yet, they wondered who could be knocking on their door. When they opened the door, they were more than surprised to find an elderly, diminutive Hispanic woman on their step. They were even more surprised when, without any greeting or introduction, she spoke these words:

"You need to get out! I used to live here in this old house, back when it was just a farm and I was a little girl. There is something very evil here. This place is haunted and you need to get out!" The woman then turned and left, never to be seen again by the Bither family.

This message would be disturbing for any new resident, but for Doris it was particularly ominous. Already on the run from a bevy of personal problems, tumultuous relationships, and inner demons, Doris couldn't help but wonder if she hadn't just made life worse for herself and her children by moving into this cramped rental. A few months after this strange woman's visit, Doris would have her answer, and it would be more horrifying than anything she could have imagined.

* * *

Doris Bither grew up in a turbulent household, the daughter of two alcoholic parents who lacked the means and motivation to give Doris and her brother a stable upbringing. When she was 10, the family moved from the Midwest to California. As she entered her teenage years, Doris became increasingly rebellious and entangled herself in drugs, alcohol, and the occult. Eventually her erratic lifestyle and raucous behavior led to her being disowned by her family. The rejection was made complete when she later learned that the total inheritance from her parents went to her brother.

Life for Doris from that point on was a continuous uphill battle. She bounced from job to job, struggled through numerous relationships and marriages, all while trying to provide for children whose fathers were out of the picture. Making matters worse, Doris continued to rely on alcohol and drugs to deal with the stresses of her everyday existence. While Doris thought she was keeping her demons at bay through self-medication, what she didn't realize was that her other pastime—dabbling in séances and Ouija boards—was sabotaging her already-hapless efforts to find peace. As stated in interviews years later with Doris's sons, subtle but steady amounts of paranormal activity, which included objects moving by themselves and frightening apparitions, plagued the family for years up to the time they moved to Braddock Drive. Unfortunately, far from offering a fresh start, life in the new house soon became a waking nightmare for Doris and her children.

At first, the events in the house were similar to what the Bither family had experienced at their other residences: dancing orbs of light, shadows in the corners, cold spots in various rooms. And while hazy apparitions were occasionally witnessed in the past, now they were more distinct, as well as more frequent. Brian Harris, Doris's middle son, years later told paranormal investigator Javier Ortega that there were four entities, human-like but translucent, "who showed themselves whenever they felt like . . . . At times, it would be annoying. We would be watching television and these things would walk by. Like nothing." Annoyance quickly turned to terror, however, as the entities increasingly displayed a malevolent streak. "We all experienced some form of attack. . . pulling, biting and scratching." Brian and his older brother recalled specifically being bumped into by nothing visible on multiple occasions, as well as being slapped awake in the middle of the night by unseen hands.

The most horrific attacks, however, were directed at Doris. She claimed that not only did the spectral beings bump into her and harass her in minor ways, but that on multiple occasions they outright sexually assaulted her. Her oldest son supposedly witnessed one of the "rapes" when he entered her bedroom upon hearing his mother's screams. To his shock, he saw her being tossed around like a doll as she appeared to be fighting off invisible attackers. When he tried to go to her aid, he was picked up and thrown against the wall by "something" he couldn't see. Middle son Brian also corroborated these claims: "The whole rape thing was real. My room was right next door to my mother's. I would hear the attacks happening. Things being thrown, her screaming. Then she would come out of the bedroom and have all these bruises. On her legs, her inner thighs." Sometimes the attacks happened outside the bedroom, in front of the children. Brian again recalled these terrifying moments: "Imagine a woman being beaten. You could see her being picked up and thrown around. Sounds, slaps...but there was no one there to actually do it."

In August 1974, during the height of this paranormal onslaught, Doris overheard a conversation in a local bookstore about haunted houses. She approached one of the speakers, who happened to be a researcher at UCLA's parapsychology laboratory by the name of Kerry Gaynor, and timidly told him that she lived in a haunted house. After listening to more of Doris's story, Kerry told her that he would consult with his colleague, Dr. Barry Taff, and arrange for a visit, if that was okay. Doris readily agreed.

The first visit to the Bither house consisted of Gaynor and Taff simply interviewing Doris and her children about the alleged paranormal activities and apparitions. Their purported claims were so incredible-sounding that the two researchers decided afterward that they would hold off with any follow-up investigation. According to Taff in a later report, their first instinct was that Doris was in need of psychiatric help. However, a few days later Doris contacted them and said some neighbors had now seen the apparitions. Intrigued, the two scientists returned to the Bither house, this time with cameras and tape recorders. Things started getting interesting pretty quickly.

Gaynor was setting up his equipment and talking to Doris's eldest son in the kitchen when suddenly a cabinet door they were standing near swung open. A frying pan flew out and followed a curved path for about two and a half feet before hitting the floor with a loud thud. After carefully examining the scene and coming up with no explanation as to how the pan flew out at all, to say nothing about in an elliptical direction, the investigators proceeded to Doris's bedroom. The first thing they noticed was the unusually low temperature in the room compared to the rest of the house. Then the smell hit them: the stench of rotting, decomposing flesh. To round off the unpleasant sensory experience, they also noted a physical sensation of "overpressure," as if their eardrums were at the bottom of a deep pool.

A friend of Doris's, a woman by the name of Candy who claimed to also be a psychic, joined Gaynor and Taff as they prepared to take a series of Polaroid camera shots in the room. Their first photo of the bedroom turned out perfectly normal. But a few minutes later, Candy shouted that she sensed something in the corner. Taff immediately pointed the camera in that direction and fired off a shot. The resulting photo was completely bleached white as if, Taff speculated, it had been "exposed to some powerfully ionizing radiation." About fifteen minutes later, Candy again shouted out that there was something in the corner of the bedroom. Once again Taff snapped his camera, and once again the photo came out bleached. To make sure the camera itself was working correctly, Taff took a photo of a different area of the room — one where Candy did not sense a presence — and the result was a normal-looking picture.

The next photo that Taff took was of the closed bedroom door. This shot proved the most interesting to this point, as it clearly showed a one-foot-in-diameter ball of light hovering near the bottom of the door. None of the people gathered in the room saw the light at the time the photo was taken, but minutes later, all in the room became witnesses to zig-zagging electric-blue balls of light near the bedroom's window. Taff immediately snapped his Polaroid at the dancing balls, but was disappointed to see another bleached and blurry result. The glowing, bluish lights slowly faded, and minutes later Candy announced that something was standing directly in front of her. This time Gaynor took up the camera and fired off a shot. The resulting photo showed no mysterious being and was, in fact, quite sharp in its display of other objects in the room, including the intricate patterns on the curtains and those on Candy's dress. What wasn't sharp was Candy's face; it was completely erased by the same type of bleaching effect seen in previous photos. About two minutes later, after Candy said the "presence" was gone, Gaynor took another picture of her. This time the photo came out perfectly normal with no bleaching or blurriness anywhere.

Over the next six weeks, Gaynor and Taff, along with varying numbers of lab assistants and students, made weekly visits to the Bither house. At the third and fourth sessions, the predominant phenomena they observed were pulsating lights that jetted around Doris's bedroom in varying sizes and intensities. At times, the lights acted like three-dimensional holograms, undulating, expanding, and contracting until they encompassed the entire corner of the room. Though numerous attempts were made to photograph the lights, only a few captured anything at all, and at best showed a blurry orb with no contextual background suitable for analysis.

At one of the visits, Doris's sixteen-year-old son told the investigators that the lights responded to certain record albums that he liked to listen to. The albums, by Black Sabbath and Uriah Heep, contained a couple of songs dealing with devil worship that in particular seemed to "infuriate it," her son said. Taff decided to test this himself, and wrote concerning his findings: "Much to our surprise, when the records were playing the songs indicated by Doris's son, the anomalous light activity dramatically increased, reaching a crescendo in conjunction with the music, in fact, with specific passages within each of the two songs."

The fifth session at the house began with the investigators putting up black poster boards on the walls and ceilings of Doris's bedroom, each board numbered and separated with white duct tape to form a grid network. Taff and Gaynor hoped the blackened room would more readily illuminate the light phenomena, and that the grid would serve as a reference for attempted photographs. In addition to the two lead scientists, thirty other individuals from the UCLA parapsychology laboratory were present. Crammed into Doris's tiny bedroom, awaiting the paranormal light show, the audience was soon rewarded. Not only did the lights return, more brilliant than ever thanks to the darkened environment, but they seemed to demonstrate a direct responsiveness to verbal suggestions. In particular, when Doris yelled and cursed at the lights (as she assumed they represented the entities that had been attacking her), they appeared as a bright lime green and intensified to a larger degree than any others.

At this point, Taff and Gaynor initiated a more controlled experiment in an attempt to establish communication with whatever unseen force was in the room. They asked aloud for "it" to respond to their questions by blinking out yes and no answers on the numbered black poster boards: two blinks (flashes) in panel three for "yes" and four blinks in panel six for "no." To the amazement of all gathered, the lights started responding immediately to the asked questions, putting out sharp and fast flashes of light on the selected boards, which indicated to Taff "that we may have been dealing with some type of incorporeal or discarnate intelligence."

Though multiple photographs were taken of the night's events, none exactly showed the flashing balls of light that witnesses saw with their naked eyes. What appeared instead in the pictures were bright arcs of light. The most spectacular arc appeared over Doris as she was sitting on her bed. Others were seen floating in the middle of the room. Taff believed the cameras' shutter speeds were not fast enough to capture the movement of the rapidly moving spheres and thus resulted in their appearance as tracks, or time-lapse photos. When the photo of the rainbow-shaped arc over Doris was shown later to Adrian Vance, an editor of *Popular Photography* magazine, Vance maintained there was no situation or setting that could have produced an inverted arc like that, given the nature of optical glass in a 35mm SLR camera.

Their experiments and observations completed for the evening, Taff and Gaynor believed they were done at Doris's house until their scheduled visit the following week. But the next evening, Doris called in a panic, claiming that "all hell" had broken loose that afternoon and asking if the two scientists could come over immediately. When Taff and Gaynor arrived at the house later that night, they were told that the house had "come alive" with paranormal activity that included attacks by spectral entities, flying pots and pans, and last but not least, the ripping down of the black poster boards in Doris's bedroom. As they took a look in the bedroom, the investigators were greeted once again by an overwhelmingly foul stench and the presence of a penetrating cold. They examined the torn-down panels and noted with curiosity that the boards and their industrial-strength tape were torn down with such force that large portions of plaster were removed as well.

Five days later, Taff and Gaynor returned to the Bither household with multiple assistants and volunteers. As in previous sessions, a séance was conducted to summon whatever entities might be present. The response was immediate: a brilliant display of three-dimensional lights that once again appeared to respond to Doris's vocalizations, the emotions of the gathered crowd, and the playing of the Uriah Heep and Black Sabbath albums. The pulsating lights were so bright and piercing at this session that everything in the room was illuminated: walls and ceilings, the clothes of the bystanders, and the metallic frames of the cameras. Though nine cameras were firing pretty much continuously during the light performance, all of the negatives turned out clear. What kind of light, Taff wondered, reflects off solid objects, cast shadows, is visible to the naked eye, and yet does not pass through a camera lens to expose the film?

The most spectacular manifestation that took place in the house that night, though, was when at one point the lights came together to form a three-dimensional image of the upper half of a very large, muscular man. Though the apparition's torso, arms, and head were readily discernible, its facial features were undefined. More than twenty people present saw the phantasm, two of whom fainted at the sight and chose never to work with Taff and Gaynor again.

When the researchers returned a week later for their seventh session at the Bither residence, Doris and the children claimed that the night before "all hell" had again broken out in the house. A pair of candelabras had flown across the room, Doris said, and struck her on the arm. She showed Taff a large red bruise on her forearm while her son corroborated the story, saying one of the candelabras had almost hit him on its way to his mother. The two also related to Taff how a wooden board that had been firmly nailed on the wall beneath a bedroom window had been torn from its position and flung across the room by unseen hands, again narrowly missing Doris's son.

In his interview with Javier Ortega thirty-five years later, Brian Harris talked about the chaos that ensued whenever Taff and his team completed a session. "When the team would show up, I hated it; because I knew as soon as they left, they would become so angry that the house would come alive!" When pressed to explain further, Harris said, " . . . it was as if the ghosts were upset that we went and told . . . so things would start flying, we would get attacked."

In addition to throwing objects at people, the "ghosts" had ripped down, once again, the black poster boards that the investigative team had replaced the preceding week. Because the thought had crossed their minds that Doris or her kids had torn down the boards, Gaynor asked during the weekly séance for the entities to show their strength by tearing down the boards in the investigators' presence. The response was immediate and amazing.

Within five seconds of the request, several of the poster boards on the ceiling directly above Doris's head were torn loose, dropping swiftly down on the surprised woman's head. The boards on the wall were targeted next, their tape peeled back by unseen hands and the boards either left to drop or flung across the room. In addition to Gaynor and Taff, those who witnessed this incredible display included various lab assistants, several psychiatrists, and the head of the UCLA parapsychology laboratory, Dr. Thelma Moss.

The eighth and final visit a week later proved disappointing to the investigators. They detected only a faint odor and slight cold in the bedroom, saw no spectacle of lights, nor any manifestations of any kind. Taff noticed there was a difference in Doris's demeanor during this visit, as well as the last. She was much less belligerent, vocal, or even fearful toward the entities in the house. It was as if, he noted later, she had given up or just didn't care anymore. The diminished paranormal activity that coincided with Doris's calmer disposition, as well as the increased activity witnessed when Doris was upset or antagonistic, fueled Dr. Taff's theory that the "poltergeist" phenomena observed in the Bither household were largely caused by Doris herself, the result of unconscious telekinetic abilities. He allowed, however, for the possibility that there might have been a "discarnate intelligence" involved as well, working in concert, perhaps, with Doris's own mind.

Interestingly, in 2008 Taff updated his conclusions about Doris's case. Citing more than 30 years of additional research and 3,500 investigated cases, he rejected his earlier notion of a discarnate intelligence or other independent spectral agent being involved and instead labeled the case "one of extreme RSPK" or Recurrent Spontaneous Psychokinesis.

According to parapsychologists and other professionals who study paranormal events, telekinetic or "psychic energies" are often associated with individuals, usually young people, who are experiencing extreme stress and, knowingly or not, internalize their problems until there is such a build-up of energy that it materializes in externally forceful and disturbing ways. Even some clergy members acknowledge this theory as a credible explanation for many poltergeist ("noisy ghost") occurrences. In a 2017 interview with the South Wales Argus newspaper, Anglican bishop and exorcist Dominic Walker said: "We don't believe it's a ghost but is a psychic energy produced by someone which causes things to move about." He then recounted a case he witnessed himself: "I saw a jar of coffee come flying out of the kitchen and things had tumbled over. Then a pot plant just fell over. There was no clear explanation and the people involved were very upset. It was quite scary. We later discovered that there was a youngster going through a difficult time and needed to talk. Then once the person spoke of the trauma and it was resolved, it all died down."

Unfortunately in Doris Bither's case, neither her external nor internal problems went away so easily. Shortly after Taff and his team finished their investigation, Doris moved her family from Culver City to Carson, California. She contacted Taff about three months later to tell him she was still experiencing paranormal phenomena but at a greatly reduced level. Taff's contact with Doris became very infrequent after that, but he learned enough through the years to know that she moved several more times, from Carson to San Bernadino, then to Texas, and then back to California. Her unstable lifestyle still included large amounts of alcohol and multiple boyfriends. At one point, she told Taff that one of the "spirits" (who had supposedly followed her to every location) had impregnated her, but there were never any official records found that showed a pregnancy or birth. In 1999, Doris died at the age of 59 of respiratory failure. Her son Brian, who was with her at the time, reported seeing dancing balls of light in her room right before she passed.

Because Doris had no interest in looking at her problems from a spiritual point of view, and because Taff and members of his team followed a purely scientific methodology, it is not on record that Doris ever received help from any clergy in the form of deliverance rituals or exorcisms. It may not have helped anyway if indeed Dr. Taff's theory was correct and Doris's "haunting" was all in her mind. But just as there are clergy who accept the telekinesis explanation for poltergeist activity, there are others who warn that the typical phenomena associated with such—objects moving about by themselves, lights and appliances turning on and off, doors opening and closing, putrid smells, random temperature drops, disembodied voices, and even physical attacks—are also classic signs of demonic infestation and oppression. This is particularly true if the targeted victim had prior involvement in the occult, as did Doris with her early obsession with the Ouija board and séances. As London exorcist Father Jeremy Davies notes: "Poltergeist phenomena are often said to be due to psychological tension in a member of the household; but when there is occultism in the history or some sort of evil threat is apparent, there is probably a demonic element." It is hard to argue that Doris and her children were not under an "evil threat." The slaps, pushes, bites, and sexual assaults they claim happened to them go way beyond the actions of boisterous spirits.

Perhaps the best explanation for Doris Bither's strange and incredible narrative is one posited by Jesuit priest Herbert Thurston (1856-1939), who was regarded as an expert on the spiritualist movement and occult phenomena. After investigating scores of poltergeist hauntings himself, he offered this conclusion:

"That there may be something diabolical, or at any rate evil, in them I do not deny, but, on the other hand, it is also possible that there may be natural forces involved which are so far as little known to us as the latent forces of electricity were known to the Greeks. It is possibly the complication of these two elements which forms the heart of the mystery."

The Doris Bither case inspired Frank De Felitta's 1978 book The Entity, which was made into a film of the same name in 1982 starring Barbara Hershey.

Trapped by the Occult

Jan had everything going for her. She was young, attractive, and soon-to-be-married. Her fiancé, Derek, with whom she lived, was a successful businessman who owned his own financial consulting business as well as several thriving rental properties. She and Derek were the envy of their friends, but Jan was not as content and carefree as she appeared. She wanted more out of life than just being Derek's girlfriend or wife. She liked the prosperity that being with Derek brought, but she longed for something deeper. Something that would make her knowledgeable, gifted, and empowered. Something that would help her understand the very meaning of life.

While Jan considered herself open-minded, there was one thing she had no time for: organized religion. So in her quest to find her path to self-fulfillment, she starting exploring the occult, something as far removed from established churches as she could find. She had been introduced to this alternate realm a few years back by her brother, a Wiccan who practiced primarily "white" magic but who at times was known to delve into the darker aspects of witchcraft. Jan wasn't sure that she wanted to follow her brother's exact path. She wanted to find the truth—whatever that was—by her own means.

With that intent in mind, she set out one morning for an occult book and paraphernalia shop she had seen advertised in the local paper. The shopkeeper was very amiable and recommended some books to Jan, set her up with some ritual candles, and then handed her a business card with a phone number scribbled on the back. This group, the shopkeeper said while pointing to the number, was made up of actual "practitioners" who would be happy to guide Jan in her quest for hidden truths. They were very friendly, she stressed, and quite open to newcomers.

The group, which loosely called itself a coven, was comprised of individuals who were devotees of various psychic arts, meditation systems, and other occult practices, including witchcraft. True to the shopkeeper's word, the group did indeed welcome Jan with open arms. Over the next several months, Jan faithfully attended the weekly gatherings, absorbing everything the group had to offer. At one meeting, the members sat in a circle and did a guided meditative journey. Jan remembered turning ice-cold during the session, though the room itself was warm. Afterward, some of the participants came up to Jan and told her they saw animal-like figures surrounding her during the meditation.

As Jan became more involved with the coven, she started experiencing some strange phenomena at home. She would see shadows dart about, usually from the periphery of her vision. She also started hearing whispering when she was alone, and not just from a single voice but from multiple, as if a conversation among ghosts was going on. As these occurrences became more frequent, Jan quit the coven for fear that she was bringing "something" home with her. But she continued her occult research, hoping the books she turned to would help her understand the nature of these disturbances and how to deal with them. Unfortunately, things only got worse despite Jan's extensive reading. The moving shadows and disembodied voices continued, but now lights were flashing on and off by themselves, windows were opening and closing, and the telephone was ringing in the middle of the night with no one on the other end.

Disturbances were also happening in Jan's relationship with Derek. He couldn't understand Jan's fascination with the occult. To him, it was all a bunch of time-wasting nonsense. The couple began arguing more and more, much of it over trivial matters, and they found themselves seeking more time away from each other than together. Rather than just let the relationship die naturally, Jan gave in to her anger and resentment toward Derek and used a ritual she learned in one of her books to put a curse on him. The curse was designed to make the recipient suffer, not in a physical sense, but by losing wealth and wellness of mind. A few months later, Derek saw his business collapse, and after a violent altercation fueled by stress and uncertainty, he split from Jan for good.

Jan was devastated that Derek had actually left. Incredibly, as if a fog had settled over a part of her mind, she didn't believe that her "silly little spell" had anything to do with Derek's actions. It wasn't until she began feeling and seeing scratches appear on her skin for no apparent reason that Jan started to make the connection between her occult dabblings and all the negative things that had been happening in her life. A concerned friend whose uncle was a Catholic priest put Jan in touch with the clergyman. After an investigation into Jan's background, he concluded that her occult practices had brought demonic forces into her life and arranged for an exorcism to be performed.

For the next ten years after the exorcism, Jan enjoyed a relatively normal life. She had a steady job, a new house, and a six-year-old daughter, Amy, from a short but intense relationship. She also had a new man in her life, Brandon, a hard-working contractor who showered Jan and Amy with devotion and provided the security Jan had quietly been craving those years on her own. When Brandon sold his condo and moved in with Jan, the future seemed bright for the happy couple. Marriage, children, and successful careers all seemed imminently doable. That is, until uninvited visitors from Jan's past showed up.

Jan first noticed the disturbances a few weeks after Brandon moved in. Fleeting shadow figures that disappeared into walls as quickly as they appeared. Objects that went missing or were moved to new locations. Whispered voices when Jan was all alone. At first, it was only Jan who experienced these things. Brandon worked long hours, so his time at home was limited, and, as he was new to the house, he really wouldn't have noticed if something was out of place. But that was all soon to change.

Brandon lay in bed one night with thoughts of his mother's upcoming birthday party running through his head. Trying to get comfortable, he turned away from Jan and toward the window. There in plain view was a sight he'd never forget. Silhouetted against the window stood a black figure wearing what looked like a monk's robe and cowl. While he couldn't make out any facial features under the deep folds of the hood, Brandon felt as if the figure was peering at him intently. Part of his brain told him to get up and confront whoever it was, but a stronger part held him frozen in place with the knowledge that this wasn't a human intruder in his room. After what seemed an interminable amount of time, the figure finally faded into the dimness. When he was certain that the entity was gone, Brandon got up and went to the kitchen for a drink. He decided to keep the incident to himself so as to not upset Jan, unaware that Jan had already been witnessing paranormal events herself.

In fact, Jan's experiences were intensifying. One particularly frightening event happened while she was home alone and in the basement washing clothes. As she attended to the laundry, she saw in her periphery vision multiple black shapes circling her. Whenever she turned to look at them straight on, they vanished from her sight. This went on several times until, finally finished with her chores, she turned to go back upstairs, her nerves severely frayed at this point. Suddenly, a stench permeated the basement unlike anything Jan had ever experienced. She would later reflect that it was like a combination of rotting eggs and decaying flesh, but at that moment it so strongly assaulted her senses that she doubled over, gagging and retching. She forced herself up the stairs, nearly tripping when the light bulb over the washing machine unexpectedly blew out. As she closed the basement door and leaned her back on it, gasping for fresh air, she vowed to never go back down there unless someone else was in the house with her.

A couple of weeks after his first encounter with the shadow being, Brandon came home late from work and, as was his habit, first went to check on Jan in the bedroom before having a snack in front of the television. He quietly pushed open the door and immediately froze. Hovering around Jan while she slept were multiple black, hooded figures. Brandon's pulse quickened and sweat gathered on his brow as he recalled the entity that had appeared to him. He was shocked not only by how many were present but also by how their presence alongside Jan seemed sexual in nature. Brandon backed up slowly into the hallway to gather his courage, then, taking a deep breath, he slammed open the door and flicked the light switch on the wall. The shapes vanished.

Jan recalled nothing out of the ordinary the next morning when Brandon asked her how she had slept, but she did have her own unsettling experience later that day. She was setting the table for dinner when she glanced toward the living room and noticed something odd. The framed photos she had on an end table were all face down. She knew they weren't like that an hour ago when she was in that room reading. She picked them up and inspected each for damage. They all appeared to be fine, until she looked at the last one, a picture of her and Amy and Brandon. Brandon's face and chest had been scratched out. Everything else in the picture was perfectly intact.

Jan started feeling like her life was once again spiraling out of control. She was wracked with guilt that she had somehow attracted these *things* back into their lives, but she had no idea how. She had not dabbled in anything related to the occult for years, nor did Brandon as far as she knew. Yet all this new trouble seemed to have originated when Brandon moved in. Did he unknowingly bring something with him?

Regardless of where it came from, the disturbing activity in the house was picking up speed. Almost every day now, either Jan or Brandon experienced something. Cabinet doors opening and closing by themselves, lights flickering on and off, objects going missing, putrid smells filling a room, cold spots throughout the house, phantom voices whispering unintelligibly. And, of course, the shadows. Jan saw them constantly out of the corners of her eyes, swirling and darting, almost materializing but never quite. Brandon, on the other hand, continued to see the shadows in their more terrifying form: featureless human-like figures. Up until this point, Brandon had only seen the shadow people at night, which was bad enough. But one afternoon he was talking to Jan and looked past her to see a black form standing in the doorway of his office. It was the size of a small man and had the basic shape of a human, but there was a grotesqueness to it that made Brandon's skin crawl. It vanished in thin air within seconds.

Brandon could no longer keep what he had been seeing to himself. He sat Jan down and told her about the shadow

Trapped by the Occult

figures he had been seeing since his first days in the house. He expected her to treat him like he was crazy, but instead he listened with amazement as Jan told him every strange and scary thing that had happened to her as well. Jan also confessed to her earlier involvement in witchcraft and the occult and how that had led to similar disturbances years ago. Teary-eyed, she begged Brandon to forgive her for not telling him earlier; she had only been trying to protect him, she said. She truly believed that if she just ignored those *things* when they first started, if she didn't give them any attention or energy, that they would go away. She realized now how foolish that assumption had been. After much more discussion and tears, they both agreed that they needed help.

* * *

John Zaffis is a paranormal investigator who has responded to thousands of reports of supernatural happenings throughout the United States and many other parts of the world. He has written books, appeared on television shows, and conducted lectures at universities throughout the country. With over 40 years of experience, he is sometimes referred to as the "Godfather of the Paranormal." John was recommended to Jan and Brandon during their search for help, and he wasted no time coming out to see the desperate couple.

In his first interview with Jan and Brandon, John discovered that Jan's brother, Chris, may have had more of an influence on her present situation than previously believed. Jan revealed that after Derek had left her years ago, she moved in with Chris for a few weeks. Chris had a very controlling personality, Jan explained, and had always wanted to be the "superior" sibling. Consequently, he reveled in Jan's failures and became jealous of her successes, which included her relationships with other men.

87

One night, Chris insisted that Jan participate in a candle magic ritual designed to bind dark spirits that were afflicting one of Chris's friends. Jan declined but remained on the side and watched as Chris performed the ritual inside a drawn circle surrounded by multicolored candles. Chris's behavior was so frantic and bizarre during the ceremony that Jan asked him, unsuccessfully, to stop several times. When he was done, Chris told Jan that during the ritual he had seen several small, dark animal-like creatures in the room with them. Too bad Jan hadn't been in the circle with him, he said. Then she would have seen them too. Jan was glad she hadn't been in that circle, and a week later she moved out.

John speculated that Jan's brother could be partially responsible for her paranormal troubles simply by practicing his dark arts in her presence, or, more disturbingly, by perhaps sending a curse or attachment her way in order to dominate her. Jan agreed it could be possible.

What troubled John most about this case was the increasing hostility the entities were exhibiting toward Brandon. After some initial hesitation, Jan told John about a recent incident that backed this concern. Jan and Brandon had retired to their bedroom and were beginning to get intimate when Jan noticed several dark shapes hovering around Brandon. Though it was dark in the room, these figures were unmistakably vivid, as they were darker than the blackness in the room. As their lovemaking continued, Jan became concerned that Brandon wasn't reacting to her words or actions. He was also being unusually rough. It was like he was in a trance, she told John. The shapes remained around Brandon until both he and Jan fell asleep.

In another incident that further worried John, Jan admitted to actually "siccing" the beings in the house on Brandon after an intense argument one night. According to

Jan, Brandon came home late one night from visiting his mom. Already stressed from everything that had been happening in their home, Jan flew off the handle. She demanded to know why he had been spending so much time at his mom's. Was he even at his mom's, or somewhere else? Soon the two of them were in a full-fledged fight. After an hour of shouting and cursing at each other, Brandon stormed out of the house. Driven by a spirit of rage, Jan ordered whatever was in the house to go after Brandon and "get him."

John knew that Jan didn't truly wish harm upon Brandon. In his experience, this was one of the realities of being oppressed by evil spirits: the mental and physical stress of dealing with a constant barrage of paranormal phenomena will often result in strained relationships, verbal abuse, physical violence, or even self-harm. In this case, John believed the ultimate goal of these nefarious beings was to get rid of Brandon so they could have Jan for themselves. What better way than to cause bitterness and anxiety between the couple until a breaking point was reached?

John knew what had to be done to rid the dark forces from Jan and Brandon's life, but he also suspected his recommendation would be met with a less-than-enthusiastic response. The reality was that they were up against a negative, evil entity. Everyone agreed on that. To counteract it, they needed to invoke a positive, pure force, or, in John's words, "a higher spiritual power." He explained to them: "You can fight as long and hard as you like, but these things that plague you have the upper hand. They respond to religion and this appears to be the only way to rid them from your life."

Jan and Brandon were fine with the idea of a one-time religious ritual like a blessing or exorcism. After all, Jan had that done a decade ago and it seemed to work. John reminded them, though, that the demons came back, if they had ever left at all. These entities can lay dormant for years, he explained, as time doesn't have the same meaning for them as it does for us. But the most likely reason the exorcism didn't "take," John surmised, was because Jan didn't make the necessary changes in her life to repel the evil. "The real change needs to take part on your behalf. You need to fight it with a positive outlook and faith." The idea of going to church didn't settle well with the couple. Brandon was a lapsed Catholic, and Jan, of course, had a distaste for traditional religion for as long as she could remember. They agreed to think about John's advice.

It was several months later when John came back to the house for a follow-up interview. Things had not gotten better; in fact, they had taken a turn for the worse. Brandon was in the hospital, recovering from a serious fall that they feared could leave him paralyzed. The strange disturbances and shadow figures still plagued them. And their emotional stress was to the point of despair. When Jan related what they had been doing since John's last visit, he wasn't surprised that they had gotten themselves into deeper trouble.

Rejecting John's recommendation to embrace a positive, faith-based lifestyle, yet desperately wanting to rid themselves of their terrifying situation, they turned to the very thing that started the demonic oppression in the first place: the occult. Jan had tried "cleansing" the house using several homegrown rituals. They had reached out to psychics, ghost hunters, and other paranormal investigators with no success. Then Brandon heard about a local Santerian priestess who supposedly could "broker deals" with troublesome otherworld entities. (Santeria is a pantheistic religion originally practiced in Cuba that merges the worship of certain West African deities with Catholic saints.) Perhaps, Brandon thought, this was the practical, tangible solution they were looking for. He met with the priestess and, true to her reputation, she offered him a deal, but it would cost him one of three things: his eyes, his ears, or his legs. Brandon agreed to paying with his legs, hoping this part of the deal was more symbolic than anything else.

He couldn't have been more wrong.

Shortly after meeting with the priestess, Brandon went out one day to the mailbox. Before he made it back to the front door, he collapsed in agony. He felt like someone had taken a baseball bat to his lower back, except that no one was around. Jan came running out upon hearing his screams and called an ambulance. While they waited for it to arrive, Brandon writhed in pain on the ground, unable to move from the spot where he had fallen. At the hospital, doctors determined that discs in his lower back had been crushed, but how remained a mystery. Moreover, the trauma had caused fluids to be released which could lead to partial paralysis, if not the worst-case scenario of Brandon never walking again.

John was deeply saddened to hear about this latest development. But what saddened him the most, apart from the terrifying physical attack on Brandon, was the couple's refusal to do what was necessary. Even as Brandon lay in pain in a hospital bed, neither he nor Jan was willing to consider a religious remedy. Instead, they continued to hope the "problem" would go away on its own or that they would eventually hit upon the right magical incantation that would give them a quick fix and allow them to go on living their normal lives.

But there would be no more normal, John insisted, if Brandon and Jan didn't completely renounce all ties to the occult—past, present, and future. As long as any of those elements remained in their lives, the couple would never be free. Once these entities—call them what you will: demons, evil spirits, negative energies—get a foothold into your life, they will never settle for anything less than total dominance.

This is especially true when someone invites them in, as Jan did by dabbling in the occult in her younger years and, more directly, by putting curses on her ex-boyfriend, Derek, and her current boyfriend, Brandon.

As John had seen time and time again, once the trap has been set and the victims entangled, the oppressors will use their prey like puppets, directing them in ways that makes their lives a never-ending struggle. Many people escape, but many others don't and are brought to a low emotional state of such fear and despair that suicide is often seen as the only way out.

Another very real, horrific outcome of not using the proper means to fight against these dark forces is full-blown demonic possession. When John spoke to Jan and Brandon for the last time, he feared that both of them were very near this point. "I feel that if an exorcism was performed," John stated later, "it would have been performed over both of them. There was definitely the possibility of an entity coming through either of them."

It is unknown at the time of this writing if Jan and Brandon ever found their way out of the darkness. They were heading down a dangerous path when John first met them and sliding down it even faster when he left. One can only imagine what was waiting for them at the bottom.

The Infestation

As a young boy growing up in Pittsburgh, Bob Cranmer used to stand outside the stately Craftsman-style house at 3406 Brownsville Road and imagine someday being inside it, maybe even owning it. The house's ornate architecture—its leaded glass windows, large white pillars, and decorative woodwork—made the house appear like a castle. Rumors of it being haunted didn't phase him. How could anything so beautiful be bad?

It was quite a twist of fate, then, when over twenty years later Bob discovered the house was for sale right after he and his young family moved back to Pittsburgh following his tour of duty in the U.S. Army. Even more surprising, or fortunate, as Bob thought of it at the time, was the acceptance of his lowball offer. Not only did the current owners accept his bid of $20,000 less than the asking price, but they seemed extremely anxious to move out. When Bob asked if there was anything wrong with the house, he received this odd response: "No, no, the house is great . . . . We even celebrated Mass in the house a few times."

On December 12, 1988, Bob and his wife, Lesa, and their four children moved in, still incredulous that the stately mini-mansion with nine-foot ceilings, six fireplaces, built-in bookcases, a dedicated music room, and a wraparound second-floor balcony was actually theirs. But their dream house soon revealed that it was neither a dream nor theirs. The very first indication that something was wrong came when they were looking around the property shortly before moving in and found their 3-year-old son, Bobby, standing on the staircase sobbing and hyperventilating. Though the boy was clearly terrified, he couldn't articulate what had scared him so badly. Nothing out of the ordinary was visible to anyone else.

A few months after settling in, the family started experiencing other strange phenomena. Particularly unnerving to Bob and Lesa was the sensation of being watched constantly by someone or something that they couldn't see. Whatever it was, it filled them with a sense of dread and the uneasy feeling that something wasn't right with the house. Soon other, more tangible, paranormal events occurred. Lights and faucets turned on and off by themselves, cups tipped over on their own, the radio came on without anyone touching it, and personal items frequently went missing or were oddly misplaced. Bob explained in later interviews that while these events were a bit unsettling at first, the family got used to them and accepted the idea of living with a "spirit" in the house. When a plate slid off the table on its own, someone would simply pick it up and move on.

This curious co-existence went on for many years before the "spirit" intensified its activities and exposed the Cranmers to new and frightening phenomena that included loud pounding on walls and floors, heavy footsteps heard roaming about the house, furniture moving on its own, pictures on walls rotating, and mysterious blood-like streaks appearing high on the walls of certain rooms. (When Bob had one of the streaks tested by a lab, the results were inconclusive as to the origin of the substance. The test did find, however, that the substance contained human skin cells.) The activity was becoming more violent as well, with frequent smashing and breaking of fragile items. Particularly disturbing to the Cranmers was finding a crucifix on the floor that had been bent into a grotesque L shape.

While these events and many others took place throughout the whole house, one room was consistently problematic, a second-floor bedroom the Cranmers called the "Blue Room," so named because of its blue wallpaper and blue carpet. Over the years, it served as the bedroom for multiple family members, including Bob and Lesa, but no one ended up staying in it for very long. The very atmosphere in the room was heavy and ominous, and all who occupied it were eventually subjected to the vision of a black, shadowy entity whose presence was announced by a foul stench akin to the mix of burning rubber and sulfur.

In the early 2000s, this mysterious shadow figure began manifesting outside the Blue Room. On one occasion, Bob saw it materialize as a human-shaped dark cloud, and on another it appeared as a hooded, faceless specter, reminiscent of the Grim Reaper. One of its most frightening appearances was when Bob's son-in-law saw it looming over one of the children's beds. Upon being seen, it scurried away into a dark crawlspace and vanished. On another occasion, Bob's two-and-a-half-year-old grandson suddenly started shrieking one night from the second floor. When Bob ran up the stairs, he found little Collin standing outside the Blue Room "shaking like a leaf and gasping for air." Collin pointed to inside the room and panted, "Monster, monster will get me!" The apparitions usually ended with the shadow figure disappearing into a corner of the room, after which the family would hear noises in the walls and crawlspaces as if something was moving around in them.

During this period when the apparitions were occurring more frequently and other, stronger paranormal phenomena were happening, Bob took measures in his own hand to try to thwart or banish the sinister spirit from his house. The Cranmer family had for some time now recognized that whatever they were dealing with was no longer a harmless curiosity but rather something evil and dangerous. To that end, Bob encouraged his family to pray frequently, alone and together; he walked around the house reading aloud from the Bible; and for one seven-month period, he played the movie *The Passion of the Christ* on an endless loop in a DVD player in the Blue Room. At least once or twice a week, Bob would find that either the television or the DVD player had been turned off. A few times, the DVD itself was actually removed from the player.

In late 2003, after several incidents in which family members woke up with scratches, bruises, bites, and claw marks, Bob finally reached out for help. "This thing was out to hurt us," he stated in an interview years later. The Mayor of Pittsburgh at the time, Tom Murphy, was a personal friend, and he, in turn, reached out to the Bishop of Pittsburgh, Donald Wuerl, to ask for assistance from the Catholic Church. Bishop Wuerl agreed and assigned Father Ron Lengwin to manage the Cranmer case.

As often happens when religious authorities become involved in cases of demonic activity, the demons retaliate by upping their attacks. The Cranmer case was no different. Crucifixes were broken off of rosaries, crosses flung from walls, and religious jewelry snatched right off of necks. Getting any work done in the house became a challenge, as computers routinely froze, clocks stopped running, and appliances regularly malfunctioned. Topping things off, the mysterious red streaks that had occasionally appeared on some walls in the house now were seen splattered all over.

During this time, diocesan priests regularly visited the Cranmer home to offer Masses, lead deliverance prayer services, and perform house blessings. Sometimes their actions caused the paranormal activity to settle down, other times they made it worse. As Father Lengwin explained to Bob, in order to authorize a formal exorcism, whether for the possession of a person or the infestation of a house, the bishop required examination and verification from professional sources outside the Church. To that end, he asked if Bob would allow members of the Penn State Paranormal Research Society to come to the house. If these investigators could back Bob's claims, then an exorcist could be called in. Bob was more than willing to do whatever was necessary to save his family and salvage his home.

In January 2005, Ryan Buell, the head of the Penn State Paranormal Research Society, made his first visit to the house. By the end of the visit, there was no question in Buell's mind that the Cranmers were dealing with a supernatural entity. He watched in amazement as a crucifix bent in half right before his eyes and what looked like blood appear on the walls from no visible source. Another researcher from the University, Adam Blai, recalled that the first time he entered the house, he felt a strong draw to the coat closet. He recalled it being "a gut-level, really strong feeling that there was something there." Bob told the team he had been dealing with paranormal activity in the closet for years. Nearly every day, the pull-chain on the ceiling light would become twisted around the bulb no matter how many times he unwound it and let it hang freely.

Adding further intrigue to the closet was the proclamation from a psychic on the team that there was a hidden spot in the middle of the house that they should uncover. In the back of the closet there was indeed a plastered-up wall leading to a space under the stairs. Could this be the spot? With Bob's permission, the team sawed through the plaster wall and lath boards to discover a large, musty space filled with coal dust and several other surprising items that dated back to all the previous owners of the house. Included in the find were a large amber stone, the skeleton of a small bird, three playing cards, and a sketch depicting the first owners of the house in unflattering representations. But the most intriguing item found was a Lego piece that was unmistakably from a set Bob's son Charlie used to play with as a child. How that toy got in a space that had been closed up since 1910 was a complete mystery. Bob called it "finding the demon's lair."

The bishop now had his evidence and arranged for Father James LeBar, the chief exorcist of the Archdiocese of New York, to perform the exorcism on a date set for September 2005. Leading up to the date, the Cranmers once again experienced an increased level of demonic activity. The putrid stench was everywhere in the house, and both Bob and Lesa began having bizarre, perverted dreams. One night, Bob heard a loud crash in the bathroom. He jumped out of bed and found Lesa lying on the floor and bleeding. She told him that something had pushed her into the wall with such force that it had broken her skin.

The day of the exorcism finally came. In addition to Father LeBar, three assisting priests and two laypeople arrived at the Cranmer house at 6:30 p.m. A discussion was held first about the history and nature of the infestation, and then Father LeBar went to work reciting the prayers of the ritual. The ceremony only lasted about a half-hour, and Bob was a little surprised, and disappointed, that nothing dramatic happened to signal the end of his years-long nightmare. Father LeBar was confident the exorcism had done its job, but he warned the Cranmers before he left that they should expect "echo" events to occasionally happen over the next few months. He explained that it was a phenomenon that naturally occurred after expelling a demon. He assured them it was nothing to worry about and would eventually end on its own.

About a month after the exorcism, Bob was reminded of Father LeBar's warning. While there had been no paranormal activity in the house since the ritual, some strange things started happening in the basement. Objects were being moved out of place or put directly in Bob's way as he walked from one point to another. The foul odor was back as well, though not as strong as before. Eventually, the oddities migrated to the upper house. One night Bob fell asleep holding his rosary. When he awoke, he saw that the cross had been separated from the beads and tossed across the room. Another time, right after Christmas, he went into the coat closet and found the pull-chain hanging from the light in a meticulously-formed figure eight. But when Bob saw the fleeting image of a shadow figure while adjusting the water heater, he decided a little extra help was needed to push the weakened demon out for good.

He called Father Mike Salvagna, one of the local priests who had been helping the family over the years, and arranged for a Mass to be said in the basement. On February 24, 2006, Bob, Lesa, their sons David and Bobby, and two friends gathered around a makeshift altar in the Cranmer's basement while Father Salvagna said the Mass. Throughout the service, Bob couldn't shake the feeling that they were being watched by the thing they were trying to banish. Afterward, while everyone was talking among themselves, Bob's dog started to slowly approach the entrance to the adjoining coal room. The dog then sat down and did what Bob described as a "terminal stare" into the room. Bob had seen that look by the dog before. Their adversary was in the coal room.

Bob called out to Father Salvagna and together the two men entered the room where, indeed, a faint hazy shadow was hovering in a corner. The men began praying aloud simultaneously. After several intense minutes of targeted prayers and direct commands to leave the house, the shadow dispersed and Bob could feel that the entity had "burnt itself out."

After eighteen long, bewildering years, the house at 3406 Brownsville Road, the house that Bob Cranmer had dreamt about as a boy, was finally relinquished to its rightful owners.

* * *

In his book *The Demon of Brownsville Road* (2014, Berkley), Bob claims he unearthed some historical details about the house that could explain its demonic resident. The claims are not without their skeptics, but they are interesting nonetheless. Bob asserts that:

- In 1792, a mother and her three children were killed by marauding Native Americans and their bodies buried on the land where the house stands.

- When the house was being built in 1909/1910, an immigrant laborer put a curse on the house because the owner refused to pay him money he owed.

- In the 1930s, an unscrupulous doctor used the house to perform illegal abortions, resulting in the covered-up death of at least one young mother.

Whatever the cause, or causes, of the demonic infestation at 3406 Brownsville Road, the guests that now stay there in its reincarnation as a bed and breakfast are no doubt happy that the house's past appears content to remain a historical footnote.

The Biters

The following two stories are historical accounts of two young girls who were besieged by entities that tormented them physically, notably by biting, in full view of witnesses. The stories garnered notoriety in their respective local presses and gained further-reaching recognition as members of the scientific community became involved. These cases are a little different than most of the others in this collection, as, first, there are no clear reasons why the girls were targeted; and second, by most accounts the persecutions resolved themselves. That is, the paranormal activity simply ceased after a period of time. They are nonetheless fascinating reminders that there is much in our world that neither scientists nor philosophers can explain.

Bedeviled by Dracu

On a cold February day in 1925, 11-year-old Eleonore Zugun was walking to her grandmother's house in the Romanian village of Budhai when she found, to her delight, some money on the side of the road. Not one to squander an opportunity, Eleonore spent the money on candy and quickly ate it all herself, which set off an argument with one of her cousins. Hearing the ruckus, Eleonore's 105-year-old grandmother, who was rumored by villagers to be a witch, scolded the young girl for falling for the devil's trickery. By picking up the money (which the devil had left behind, according to

Grandma), spending it on candy, and then *eating* the candy, Eleonore had ingested the devil himself and would never be free of him.

Despite these ominous words in her head, Eleonore nonetheless spent a restful night at her grandmother's and woke the next morning grateful to not be greeted by a red-eyed, fork-tailed demon sitting on her bed. But it soon became apparent that a monstrous apparition might have been the better thing to have happened that day. Shortly after breakfast, from seemingly out of nowhere, a storm of rocks came raining down on the house, battering the siding and breaking windows. Inside the house, various small objects began flying on their own toward Eleonore like projectile missiles. Convinced that Eleonore was indeed possessed by the devil, her grandmother sent her back to her home in the town of Talpa.

Three days later, all chaos broke out again around Eleonore. Rocks crashed through the glass windows, household objects sailed through the air, and doors opened and closed on their own. Eleonore's immediate family members weren't the only ones to witness these phenomena. A priest who had been called to the home watched in wonderment as a heavy trunk rocked up and down after Eleonore had sat on it. He was still speechless when, shortly thereafter, a jug of water levitated off a table. One night, a visiting family friend saw another large trunk slide across the floor on its own. The next morning, this same friend was hit in the head by a wooden spoon that flew out of a bowl of porridge.

At this point, the family and their priest decided to try an exorcism. Unfortunately, the ritual only seemed to make things worse: an iron pot exploded on the scene and several windows shattered, spraying shards of glass on family members inside

The Biters

as well as on curious villagers gathered outside. For their safety and their sanity, Eleonore's family felt they had no choice but to send her to a convent for special prayers.

This action also proved to be in vain. The nuns overseeing Eleonore reported seeing a large, heavy table levitate off the ground, as well as other unexplainable phenomena. And while it may not have been the most frightening activity to have occurred, certainly the most annoying to the nuns was having their habits transported from one cell to another, through thick walls and locked doors. Nonetheless, they continued trying to help their young charge. They had numerous Masses said on her behalf, arranged for another exorcism to be performed, and had her examined by several psychologists. But nothing abated the bizarre phenomena that surrounded her. Fearful for her safety and the safety of those around her, and on the advice of doctors who had concerns about her treatment, Eleonore's parents finally committed her to an insane asylum.

By this point, word of the strange goings-on had reached several newspapers. One such press account caught the eye of German engineer and parapsychologist Fritz Grunewald. Grunewald traveled to Talpa where he convinced Eleonore's father to bring her home from the asylum so he could study her in a friendlier environment. Eleonore came home, and Grunewald did indeed witness many instances of paranormal phenomena, including the moment a salt shaker flew off a table and struck Eleonore in the face. Intrigued by his initial findings, Grunewald resolved to study Eleonore's case more thoroughly in Germany and traveled back to make the necessary arrangements. Sadly, Grunewald suffered a fatal heart attack on that trip, leaving Eleonore once more without help or hope. Luckily, however, not for long.

Countess Zoe Wassilko-Serecki, a young Austrian aristocrat who spoke Romanian and who also had a keen interest in psychical research, had heard about Eleonore and arranged to "adopt" the girl and take her back to Vienna for formal observation. Eleonore, who had never known life outside her poor confines in Talpa, took immediately to her new surroundings. But despite her improved living arrangements and amicable relationship with the Countess, Eleonore remained at the mercy of who she now called "Dracu," the Romanian word for devil. According to Eleonore, it was Dracu who threw bottles of ink across the room, filled her shoes with water, tore up her books, destroyed her toys, and even pushed and slapped her and pulled her hair. The Countess recorded each of these events in detail and often witnessed many of them herself, including furniture moving on its own, objects dropping from the air, items transporting from one room to another, rapping on the walls, and, at least once, a strange voice making itself known.

After several months of this poltergeist-type activity, Eleonore started experiencing a new type of phenomenon— cruel and terrifying physical assaults in the form of scratches, pinpricks, and bites. The first episode happened during a séance with the countess and an acquaintance. While both her hands were being held, Eleonore suddenly cried out and claimed she had been stabbed in the arm by something sharp. At the spot she indicated, there was a small, needle-like puncture wound that appeared red and inflamed. This happened several more times during the séance until Eleonore finally refused to participate any further.

From that point on, Eleonore continued to endure painful stabbings, scratches, and, most disturbingly, bites to various parts of her body. On March 25, 1926, a professor in the mathematics department at the University of Vienna, Hans Hahn, visited Eleonore at the Countess' apartment and noted that while he held her hands, strange marks appeared on the girl's arms and hands as if she were being bitten. A few weeks later, in April, British researcher Harry Price also met with Eleonore and observed several instances of paranormal phenomena during his visit. He claimed to have seen a cushion lift itself off a chair, books fall off a shelf, a mirror transport from one room to another, and scratch marks spontaneously appear on Eleonore's face. Impressed and intrigued, Price persuaded the Countess to bring Eleonore to his National Laboratory for Psychical Research in London.

From September 30 to October 14, 1926, Price put Eleonore through an exhaustive battery of tests in his London laboratory, where he witnessed more of the unexplainable and disturbing events that he saw in Vienna, including the flight of a 10-inch steel letter opener across a room, which he firmly noted could not possibly have been thrown by Eleonore's hand. The notoriety of Eleonore's case was such that reporters and other prominent scientists were on hand to witness many of these paranormal manifestations.

Later in October in Berlin, further examination was conducted by doctors and scientists regarding Eleonore's "dermal phenomena," the term used to describe the bites and scratches that mysteriously appeared on the girl's body. Two remarkable discoveries were made. One, the bite marks on Eleonore's skin did not match Eleonore's teeth, thereby ruling out that she had bitten herself. Second, the saliva that was smeared around the piercings on Eleonore's skin did not contain the same organic material found in samples of saliva taken from her mouth. It strangely consisted of an abundance of microorganisms, many of which were staphylococci bacteria, microbes most associated with various infections.

As mysteriously as it all started, the paranormal phenomena surrounding Eleonore ceased when she reached puberty. All in all, there were a reported 3,000 instances of strange occurrences, 844 of which were seen by reliable witnesses. Peter Mulacz of the Austrian Society for Parapsychology called it an extraordinary case of psychokinesis, the movement of physical objects by the mind without the use of physical means. While many other researchers involved in Eleonore's case agreed that the power behind Eleonore's "Dracu" actually lay in the girl's own subconscious, many others admitted that it was difficult to attribute all the phenomena to this theory. Knocking books off shelves is one thing, but lifting heavy furniture that even a grown man would find taxing is quite another. Equally unexplainable by science is how an object could disappear and then reappear in a different, locked room. And then there remains the mystery of the bite marks, generated under observation by witnesses, that contained saliva proven not to be Eleonore's.

One thing was certain. To Eleonore, Dracu was real. Finally free of him after nearly three years of torture, whether because of changes in her brain or because she had given the devil his due, Eleonore gladly embraced a new and prosperous life. The Countess continued to look after Eleonore and set her up as an apprentice hairdresser. Eleonore did very well in her training, and she eventually moved back to Romania where she started a business and married. According to those who knew her, she lived a perfectly normal life and was not bothered by any further paranormal phenomena.

The Vampire Demons

Life had not been easy for Clarita Villanueva. The Filipino teenager had never known her father. Her mother, who had made a living as a fortune-telling con artist, died when Clarita was 12. Having no other family or means of supporting herself, Clarita took on low-end jobs as a maid, a dancer, and, according to some reports, a prostitute. By age 18, she was living in Manila, trying to make ends meet any way she could, often in the seedier sections of downtown. It was there, on a May night in 1953, that police arrested her for vagrancy and placed her in a 300-year-old city jail known as Bilibid Prison. Though the historical prison had been the site of countless tragedies and depravities throughout its existence, never had it experienced anything like the phenomena that was soon to center around its newest young resident.

Two days after being incarcerated, Clarita began screaming in agony. The other prisoners watched anxiously as Clarita writhed on her cot and yelled out that she was being bitten. Guards and medics rushed to her cell, where they clearly saw indentations on her skin and blood rising to the surface. The only thing they didn't see was the thing that was supposedly biting her. Finally succumbing to the invisible attack, Clarita fainted and was taken to the prison hospital. Medical personnel on duty at the time reported that they had no explanation for the mysterious bite marks.

The strange bitings continued on a daily basis, the scenario mostly the same. Clarita would scream that her tormentors were back. She would thrash around hysterically while, to the astonishment of everyone present, bite marks appeared all over her body. Father Benito Vargas, the prison chaplain, witnessed one of these assaults. He later told a reporter that although it was not his task to give an opinion, he could confirm that he saw her being bitten three times. Even more chilling was Clarita's description of her invisible attackers.

There were two of them, she claimed. The bigger one was monstrous in size, dark-skinned with curly hair all over his body. Fangs hung outside both sides of his mouth. The other one was small, only two to three feet tall, and also dark-skinned, hairy, and ugly. This little entity would climb up her body to bite her upper torso. Both of the spirits preferred to bite her, she said, on the fleshy parts of her body like the back of her legs and upper arms, as well as the back of her neck, places she obviously couldn't bite herself.

Dr. Mariano Lara, the prison's chief medical examiner, confirmed that Clarita could not have been inflicting the wounds herself. He further verified that the bite marks were too large and round (as opposed to elliptical) to be human in origin, and were wet with something akin to saliva.

News of the strange goings-on soon reached beyond the walls of the Manila prison. Major news outlets in Australia, France, Germany, England, Canada, and the United States ran headlines about the "vampire demons" and the "Draculas" attacking a young girl in the Philippines. Dr. Lara used the publicity to appeal for outside help and quickly received it.

Filipino, Chinese, and American doctors, professors, and other professionals took turns examining Clarita, but none could offer a reasonable explanation for her condition. They agreed she didn't appear to be insane, at least when she wasn't "under attack." The attacks themselves, and the bite marks that appeared before their eyes, left most of them shaking their heads. Two of the doctors, however, later speculated that Clarita was suffering from *hysteria psychoneurosis*, a mental state brought on, they argued, by the young woman's desperate need to escape her miserable current life.

The mayor of Manila, Arsenio Lacson, could no longer ignore the sensational story taking place in his city. He ordered that Clarita be brought to his office for an examination by him, a doctor, and other observers. According to some news sources, there were over 100 witnesses at the meeting, which included medical professionals, reporters, and civil authorities. The May 20, 1953, edition of the *Sydney Morning Herald* reported the events of the meeting as follows:

Mr. Lacson said that within 15 minutes while he was sitting beside her, the girl had two attacks and was bitten on her index finger and neck. She writhed and then laughed as though she had been tickled. She told the mayor the two "things" then took turns biting her neck.

Mr. Lacson said he saw marks of human teeth where the girl had been bitten.

"Clarita's hand was bitten while I was holding it," Mr. Lacson said.

"The finger was bitten under my palm. What it is is beyond me. This is something that goes way back to the dark, dim past."

He said that when the girl was asked to draw pictures of the "things," the pencil flew from her hand.

Dr. Lara, who witnessed the events in the mayor's office, commented afterward, "I always thought of this world as a visible thing but here is something unknown, a force unseen yet felt." The mayor announced that he would be asking the Archbishop of Manila to approve an exorcism on Clarita.

At this point in the timeline, official news reports of what happened after the meeting with the mayor are scarce to non-existent. There are no records indicating that an official exorcism ever took place via the Catholic Church. There was, however, a claim made by Protestant minister Lester Sumrall that he conducted an exorcism on Clarita, with the permission of Mayor Lacson, and after a three-day spiritual battle successfully freed Clarita of the demons that had been tormenting her. Sumrall, who heard about the case when it was first reported in the media, described the exorcism in his

1954 book *The True Story of Clarita Villanueva.* According to Sumrall, during the exorcism period Clarita conversed with him in English, but afterward could only speak and understand her native Filipino language.

An alternate ending to Clarita's story that makes no mention of the Reverend Sumrall came from author Frank Edwards in his book *Stranger Than Science.* Edwards, a paranormal researcher who wrote extensively for *Fate Magazine,* claims that after the meeting with the mayor, Clarita became hysterical once again during the car ride back to the prison. Everyone in the car with her, including the driver, witnessed the assault on her body. As Edwards wrote, "The fifteen-minute trip to the prison hospital was a nightmare for all involved." Once they arrived back at the jail, however, the attacks suddenly stopped. In fact, they never occurred again, according to Edwards, and Clarita began a slow but successful recovery from her terrifying ordeal.

Unconfirmed reports say that Clarita later married a rice farmer and had two children. The frustrating lack of official records or follow-up reports about her case may be due in part to the coronation of Queen Elizabeth II, which took place on June 2, 1953, and overshadowed many other news stories at the time.

Despite the conflicting accounts given by Sumrall and Edwards, as well as the sparse amount of official reports, the story of Clarita Villanueva and her "vampire demons" remains a popular horror legend in the Philippines and has even inspired a movie, the 2019 feature film *Clarita.*

Invitation to Evil

Shaylee Williams knew there was more to life than the boring confines of her rural South Dakota home. The television shows and movies she loved to watch—*Sabrina the Teenage Witch*, *Buffy the Vampire Slayer*, *Charmed*, *The Craft*—were popular with all her teenage friends, but to Shaylee they were more than simple entertainment. The characters were attractive, confident, and skilled. Their adventures hinted at the possibility of an exciting new reality that transcended the boundaries of her desolate prairie town. And even though Shaylee knew the shows were scripted fantasy and her heroes were only Hollywood actors, her interest was peaked enough that she sought every book she could find on witchcraft and the occult. As she devoured the material, she grew in the excitement of knowing she was being given the keys to a secret world, and that soon doors would open to her that she couldn't imagine. Shaylee was correct in that she would see new things. But they weren't exactly what she had in mind.

Shaylee's first experiences with the paranormal went back to her early childhood, when she would awake in the middle of the night to find an elderly Native American man sitting at the foot of her bed. There was nothing particularly scary about him, and since her family did have a partial Native American bloodline, Shaylee assumed it was a long-lost relative and went back to sleep. The idea of ghosts didn't really bother Shaylee, as several members of her family claimed to have special abilities that enabled them to see and talk to spirits. Shaylee herself remembers seeing other human spirits as a child, but she was taught by her mother not to be afraid because she could always "pray them away."

A determined teenager now, with an obsessive interest in the occult, Shaylee had no intention of getting rid of any spectral visitors. Instead, she focused on attracting them, and her efforts soon paid off. Nightly appearances of shadow people became a regular event, as did visits from the "old hag." In occult lore, the old hag is a demonic presence that sits on top of a person's chest while they are sleeping, immobilizing the victim and generating a feeling of helplessness and terror, if not outright suffocation. Modern science calls this phenomenon sleep paralysis, a state between stages of wakefulness and sleep during which a person is aware but unable to move or speak. Often the paralysis is accompanied by visions of demonic figures, the sound of whispers or voices, and an overall sense of malevolence directed toward the victim. While disturbing and often frightening, experts maintain that sleep paralysis is not dangerous or indicative of any serious condition.

While most paranormal researchers and religious exorcists accept the scientific explanation in the majority of sleep paralysis cases, there are some instances, they acknowledge, that could originate from another plane of existence. Spanish exorcist Father Jose Fortea warns that those who participate in occult rites are most at risk for night terrors, but other "innocent" people can also be attacked. Sometimes in these cases the person will awake with bruises or bite marks in places they could not have reached themselves. They will have accompanying nightmares that last for months and leave them soaking in sweat or screaming out in fear. His advice, beyond the obvious cessation of any occult practices, is to use holy water and prayer before going to bed, with the particular intention of asking for protection against demonic attacks. If the activity stops after resorting to this nightly practice, then it likely was demonic in origin. Other victims have reported that placing a cross, a Bible, the Star of David, or other religious symbols by their bed helped to reduce the attacks, or at the very least helped them feel safer falling asleep.

Unfortunately for Shaylee, she undertook none of these preventative measures but instead immersed herself more deeply in the occult even as her nighttime attacks increased in frequency and intensity. She would often feel herself pinned to the mattress, unable to move a muscle while "something" hissed with hot breath in her face. Eventually these nocturnal visits changed to a different form, the visitor this time not faceless but, as Shaylee would soon learn, just as evil.

He called himself Justin, and he was gorgeous. His youthful face was adorned with a flawless beige complexion and penetrating brown eyes; wavy dark hair fell softly upon his shoulders. He could have walked right off the cover of one of Shaylee's mom's romance novels, but rather than bare-chested, Justin always appeared in a black shirt and black pants. At first the visits were harmless; Shaylee enjoyed just being in this beautiful being's presence. But then one night she awoke in pain and panic to find Justin forcing himself on her. Shaylee later reflected that she fell into a spell of sorts, as the horror of being raped by this spectral body soon turned into the most exquisite pleasure she had ever known. He was all she could think about after that, and her obsession drove her to relish their nightly encounters, which continued for about a year.

During the day, Shaylee immersed herself in the teachings of notorious occultist Aleister Crowley and spent hours studying *The Lesser Key of Solomon*, an anonymously-written grimoire (spellbook) on demonology. She also spent more and more time with her Ouija board, delighting in her ability to use it to "call" Justin, who made his presence known by moving the planchette in figure eights. (Shaylee would learn in later years that this is a common characteristic of the demon Zozo.) Shaylee loved scaring her friends with the Ouija when they got together for sleepovers. One night she asked Justin to move the cord that hung from a ceiling lamp. Not only did the cord begin to sway but the words GET OUT were written upon the board, sending Shaylee's friends shrieking through the front door.

From reading *The Lesser Key of Solomon*, Shaylee learned about the sigils of various demons. She began drawing sigils on her body and always had one inked on the palm of her hand. Soon she grew curious if she could do more with the ritual magic symbols. A girl at school had been bullying her, so Shaylee used one of the sigils to summon a demon to go after the girl. Whether by coincidence or calculated demonic intent, the bullying girl soon experienced an "accident" that put her in the hospital.

Shaylee's delight in her apparent ability to command demons was short-lived, however, when she began to experience for herself the brunt of their malice and treachery. No longer able to control her hellish henchmen, Shaylee was kept awake at night for hours by shadow people hovering around her bed and pulling at her covers. Justin began appearing more also, but now his actions toward Shaylee were rough and hateful, leaving her with bruises and bite marks the next day. Terrified at what she had unleashed after weeks of nightly torture, Shaylee turned to her mother's faith and became a born-again Christian. Unfortunately, her sudden conversion wasn't the instant fix she had hoped for.

The day after making her private profession of faith, Shaylee met with her pastor and, upon his advice, came home and immediately threw away all of her occult books, art, and other accoutrements. She went to bed that night thinking, and hoping, that her nights of terror were behind her. She welcomed the comforting presence of her cat next to her as she drifted off to sleep. At 3:00 a.m., she was awakened by what sounded like the soft ringing of a bell. As she slowly opened her eyes and sat up, a flash of light went off, illuminating the horrific vision of a 7-foot tall figure by her door. While the black-cloaked figure had the overall appearance of a man, it was hideously disfigured, its flesh burnt and hanging like melted wax from its face, its eyes empty black sockets. The thing's arm was outstretched as it held a chain attached to a vicious-looking black dog. Shaylee sat up and tried to yell for help but her vocal cords wouldn't work. Goaded by her movement, the dog growled menacingly and yanked at its chain. Shaylee's cat leaped onto her chest, scratching her horribly. Still unable to use her voice, Shaylee recited every prayer she knew in her head, with a special invocation to the Archangel Michael. She eventually fell back onto her pillow, passing out from sheer exhaustion. When she awoke the next morning, what she remembered as being a terrible dream quickly morphed into reality when she saw dried blood on her pajamas and chest.

Shaylee has continued living her Christian faith and has reported that, while they don't happen as often, there are still times she is visited by demonic beings at 3:00 a.m. She is not harmed, she says, as she is able to "pray them away," an affirmation of her mother's advice from years ago. She wishes, of course, that the visits didn't happen at all, but accepts them as the price to be paid for her deep involvement in the occult. She warns anyone who will listen that demons are always listening for an invitation into your world. Don't give it to them, even in jest, for once they accept—and they will—they'll do whatever it takes to stay forever.

The Warlock's Curse

Susan picked at her lasagna while trying to appear interested, but in the back of her mind all she could think about was how to end this date early. She vowed she would never again agree to one of her sister's blind date setups. "He's perfect for you," Vicky had told her. "He's divorced with a kid, like you, has a great job, he's really smart. And, ooh, so good-looking."

Susan couldn't deny that Greg was good-looking. His dark hair was fashionably unkempt, his smile easy and inviting. But his eyes ... there was something about his eyes that bothered Susan. There was no reflection in them. No flickers of light or movement from the surroundings. They were just dark, lifeless orbs—pools of nothingness that were disturbingly both enticing and threatening.

But it wasn't just Greg's eyes that bothered Susan; it was also his topic of conversation.

"There are powers inside of us, Susan, incredible, mind-boggling powers that are easily within our reach with the right knowledge and tools."

"Oh? What kind of powers?" Susan asked, trying to keep up her end of the discussion.

He glanced around, then said in a low voice, "The power to get what you want."

Susan didn't like the suddenly-serious vibe Greg was giving off, so she chuckled and said, "Isn't that what vision boards are for?"

"Wishing and hoping won't get you anything," he replied after taking a sip of wine. "You have to take action. You have to take command."

"Well, sure, that's part—"

"Susan, I can make things happen to someone 500 miles away, all from the comfort of my living room. I can tell you what's going to happen tomorrow at 4:00 p.m. on the corner of 3rd and Madison. I can *make* a woman—" He paused and for a fleeting moment a look of embarrassment crossed his face. He waved his hand and smiled. "Sorry, I get intense when I talk about this stuff."

Time to put Plan B into action, Susan thought, as she nonchalantly reached into her purse. It was time to text the "save me" signal to Vicky. *Gotta keep him talking for a bit . . .*

"So, Greg, how do you do all of this? I mean, what you're telling me sounds pretty incredible."

"Simple. I command the spirits and they do my bidding."

"You command the—?"

"The spirits. Yes. It's like this: I operate on a higher plane of consciousness than most people. The spirit world, you could call it. And by serving the lord of that world, I have been given powers to control certain of its denizens."

Call, Vicky, call.

"You see, Susan, I'm a warlock."

Susan looked at him blankly. He had to be joking. Any second now he was going to say, *"Gotcha! Wow, the look on your face!"*

Only that revelation never came, just awkward silence, until, *thankfully,* Susan's phone rang.

After apologizing profusely for having to cut their date short—her babysitter was feeling sick and had to get home, *darn!*—Susan left the restaurant feeling immensely relieved that she had dodged a big bullet. Greg The Warlock would soon be nothing more than an odd footnote in her dating history.

Or so she thought at the time.

* * *

Susan spent the next day catching up on chores and spending time with her three-year-old daughter, Emma. Though the day started out pleasant, by evening dark clouds had rolled in, bringing with them wind, rain, thunder, and lightning. The racket from the storm proved too much for little Emma, who woke up screaming after a booming clap of thunder rattled the house around 11:00 p.m. Susan rushed to her room and picked the girl up, intending to bring her back to bed with her. But as she turned to leave, a strange sensation took hold of her. It started at her feet — a warm, tingling feeling that slowly rose higher up her legs, then onto her stomach, her chest, arms, and finally her cheeks. Susan tried to move but found she was rooted in place. Adding to her concern, the room had suddenly become so dark she couldn't even see Emma, though she knew the girl was still in her arms. She wondered if she was having a medical emergency of some sort, a stroke perhaps.

"Mama! Mama! Look!" Emma's urgent cry seemed to break Susan's paralysis. As the frightening numbness retreated from her body, and as her vision slowly returned to take in the dim surroundings of her daughter's bedroom, she looked to where Emma was pointing. A black, shadowy cloud hovered in the corner. It silently floated up a few feet and then, to Susan's amazement, it slowly disappeared right into the wall.

After a few minutes of being too afraid to move, even though now she could, Susan cautiously went out into the hallway. There was no sign of the black cloud or anything else out of the ordinary. She hurried into her bedroom and wrapped herself and Emma tightly under the bed covers, grateful when she finally felt the comfort of sleep come over her.

Susan woke the next morning to sunny skies, bolstering her hope that the previous night's "disturbance" was a one-time event. She told herself that it was probably a combination of the storm and stress playing tricks on her mind. Although, that didn't explain what Emma saw . . .

Susan's attempt at optimism didn't last long, as the strange numbing attack came back the next night. Like before, it started at her feet and slowly worked its way up her body, a hundred invisible fingers pushing and prodding, squeezing and groping. Making the attack more frightening was knowing instinctually that she wasn't experiencing a medical condition or mental breakdown. She was being violated by something personal, something intelligent, something malicious. Before it could completely smother her, Susan struggled with every ounce of her being to unfreeze her voice. "No," she warbled at first. Then, stronger. "No! Stop it! Go away!" To her relief, she felt the presence retreat.

For weeks the attacks continued in the night as well as during the day. Susan was now being warned of their arrival by strange whisperings and tapping noises that would occur about five minutes beforehand. Sometimes she could thwart an attack by running to the company of other people when she heard the warning sounds. But far too many times she was trapped. She couldn't say why exactly, but she had come to the definite conclusion that the phantom entity was male, an evil male. And it wanted to kill her, of this she was certain. So far, through sheer force of will, she had been able to keep it from completely suffocating her. But she felt that she was losing her strength after weeks of battle. If she lost her ability to resist . . . well, she couldn't think about that. It was too terrible.

Fearing as much, if not more, for Emma's safety as her own, Susan went for help. A divorced and lapsed Catholic, she didn't relish her appointment with the local parish priest, but she didn't know who else to go to for what was clearly a supernatural problem. To Susan's relief, Father Andrews was kindly and listened with rapt attention to Susan's story. Then he blessed her and performed what he called a "minor" exorcism on her. Susan went home feeling better than she had in weeks.

Unfortunately, her mood would soon change.

The very next day, Susan experienced another, stronger assault, as if her attacker was punishing her for seeking help. Fearing for her life now more than ever, Susan packed her things, grabbed Emma, and moved in with her sister at the other end of town. Whatever was in that house could have it, as far as Susan was concerned. She was done there.

But it wasn't the house the entity wanted. When it attacked her again the first night at her sister's, Susan knew without a doubt that this "thing" was attached to her. The big question in Susan's mind was why? What had she done to attract this invisible assailant? She wasn't even a believer in the supernatural until recently. She remembered laughing to herself the last time the subject even came up—with her blind date, Greg.

Greg The Warlock.

Susan suddenly felt sick to her stomach. Did Greg do something to her because she skipped out on their date? Put some kind of spell on her? He did say that he could command spirits. Was he commanding this one that was attacking her? It seemed ridiculous to even entertain the idea, yet at this point it made as much sense as anything else.

The next day, Susan's suspicions were confirmed in the most bizarre manner. A woman who lived in the apartment below Susan's sister intercepted her in the hallway and introduced herself as a member of the local occult community. She said she knew Greg and she knew that he had put a curse on Susan. The only way to break the curse, the woman explained, was to perform a counter-spell, which she offered to do with Susan that night at the local cemetery. Susan quickly but politely declined. She wanted nothing further to do with anything or anyone connected to Greg, even if they were offering to help. Besides, a cemetery . . .?

A week later, Susan found herself reconsidering the strange woman's offer after another attack, which this time endangered Susan's sister as well as herself.

Susan was driving home from shopping, her sister in the passenger seat, when she heard the strange whisperings that always preceded an assault. Within minutes, Susan began feeling the nightmarish numbing around her shoulders. It traveled down her back, around her waist, then back up her torso to her arms. She tried to speak but no words would come out. When she felt her fingers numbing, making it hard to hold the steering wheel, she strained to look sideways at her sister. Seeing the agonized look on Susan's face, her sister knew instantly what was happening and screamed for "it" to stop. Suddenly the car sped up as the entity pushed Susan's foot down heavy on the gas pedal. As the car swerved across the road, Susan's sister reached over and pressed the horn while screaming again at the top of her lungs. The numbing started to fade. Susan could feel the weight leave her foot, and she quickly regained control of the car. She tried to smile at her sister but a grimace was the best she could muster. They were lucky this time that the entity had retreated. But how much longer until it killed someone?

Knowing she had to do something before she and her family were put into any more danger, but still not ready to take up the occult woman's spell-casting offer, Susan reached out to paranormal investigators Ed and Lorraine Warren. The Warrens put her in touch with an exorcist, who performed a much more involved ritual than what Father Andrews had previously done. For days afterward, Susan experienced a peace she hadn't felt for months. She dared to hope that her tormentor was finally gone.

But then it came back, this time with a vengeance.

For days and nights on end, Susan was subjected to the most vicious attacks — paralysis, suffocation, molestation — until she couldn't bear it anymore. She went back to the Warrens and begged for more help. The Warrens, seeing that the usual means of relief weren't working in this case, sent Susan to an eastern mystic who had experience in dealing with evil spirits. Susan stayed with him, and whenever an attack occurred, he helped protect her. Slowly over time, the intensity of the attacks died down until they finally vanished altogether.

The curse broken, Susan lived in relative peace thereafter. Her views on the supernatural changed completely after her period of torment. No longer did she laugh at the mention of witches, warlocks, spells, and curses. She didn't laugh, but she did quickly change the subject.

Nightmare in Indiana

When major news outlets like the *Indianapolis Star*, *USA Today*, and *Inside Edition* run a story on you and your family, it would normally be considered a "big deal" and perhaps even a reason to celebrate. But for LaToya Ammons and her three children, it was not the national notoriety that was cause for celebration, but rather knowing that the nightmare described in those stories was a thing of the past. An eight-month living nightmare that, had it not been witnessed by law enforcement, health, and social services professionals, would likely still be plaguing LaToya and her family.

If it hadn't already killed them.

* * *

In November 2011, LaToya Ammons, her daughter and two sons, and her mother, Rosa Campbell, moved into a small rental house on Carolina Street in Gary, Indiana. The family barely had time to settle in before strange things started taking place, beginning with flies. Though it was nearly December and a decidedly winter chill was present, hundreds of large, black flies repeatedly swarmed the house's screened-in porch. "We killed them and killed them and killed them," LaToya's mother, Rosa, recalled, "but they kept coming back." The women also recalled a time when about two buckets-full of sand mysteriously appeared on the basement floor.

All members of the family reported hearing footsteps coming from the basement, often accompanied by the creak of the basement door opening. Sometimes the footsteps would continue even after the door was locked. One night, Rosa woke up at 3:00 a.m. and saw a shadow move past her bedroom door. She got up to investigate but found no intruder, only large, wet bootprints that looked like they came from the basement. The family was subjected to other mysterious noises as well. They frequently heard a dog growling, though neither the Ammons nor the neighbors owned a dog. At other times, they would hear knocking on the front door, but when they opened it, no one was there.

All of this was bad enough, but on March 10, 2012, the paranormal activity in the house took on a new and frightening twist. That evening, the family had company over to mourn the passing of a friend. It got to be late, after midnight, when Rosa heard LaToya call out for her: "Mama! Mama!" Rosa hurried into the bedroom where LaToya, her 12-year-old granddaughter, and a friend had been hanging out. As she entered the room, Rosa couldn't believe her eyes. Her granddaughter was levitating above the bed in a seemingly unconscious state. Alerted by the commotion, other people rushed to the room. Mother, grandmother, and their friends did the only thing they knew to do. They surrounded the girl and prayed. After several long and terrifying minutes, the girl slowly descended to the bed. She awoke right afterward but had no recollection of what had happened. The people who were visiting that night refused to return to the house.

Around this same time, LaToya's 7-year-old son was found sitting in a closet one afternoon talking to a "boy" no one could see. The phantom boy was describing what it felt like to be killed.

LaToya and Rosa knew at this point they needed help. Practicing Baptists, both recognized that they were up against something supernatural. The first couple of churches they called said there was nothing they could do. On the third try, church officials came out to the house and, after listening to the Ammons' story, agreed that they likely had spirits in their home. They told the family to thoroughly clean the house with ammonia and bleach and draw crosses on every door and window with olive oil. They suggested using the oil on the children as well.

The women also reached out to two clairvoyants who were connected to a local charismatic church. They came out with several other members of the congregation to offer their assistance and pray with the family. But it only took one trip to the basement to send the group bolting for the front door. There were 200 demons in the house, one of the clairvoyants said. The woman's parting advice: you need to move.

But moving was not an option for the cash-strapped Ammons family. Instead, LaToya took another clairvoyant's advice and put together a homemade altar in the basement. The altar consisted of an end table covered with a white sheet. On top of it were placed a white candle, statues of Jesus, Mary, and Joseph, and a Bible opened to Psalm 91. With the help of a friend, LaToya then marched through the house burning sage and sulfur in every room while her friend read Psalm 91 aloud.

You will not fear the terror of the night,
nor the arrow that flies by day,
nor the pestilence that stalks in darkness,
nor the destruction that wastes at noonday.

The Ammons' house was quiet for three days afterward. Then all hell broke loose.

LaToya's family was besieged. Particularly frightening were the random, temporary periods of "possession" that struck the mother and children. When it happened to her, LaToya recalled, she would feel lightheaded and warm. All control over her body left her and she would shake feverishly.

"You can tell it's different, something supernatural," she said. When it happened to the children—then ages 7, 9, and 12—it was even more horrifying. Their eyes bulged, their voices deepened, and evil smiles spread across their faces. The only one not affected was Rosa. In interviews, Rosa stated she believed she was born with a special protection against evil. The only time she was personally attacked was when she was in the basement one day and "something" tried to choke her.

The children bore the brunt of the attacks, both physically and mentally. Rosa recalled the time the youngest boy once flew out of the bathroom as if he'd been thrown, and another time when an unattached headboard moved on its own and bashed her granddaughter in the head, causing an injury requiring stitches. Her granddaughter later told health professionals that sometimes she felt like she was being choked and held down so she could neither speak nor move. During one of these assaults, a voice told her that she'd never see her family again and wouldn't live for another 20 minutes. All of the kids were also sick frequently, and would often wake with bloody gums, noses, and ears.

Around Easter time, the family was gathered one night in front of the television when a Fabreze bottle was lifted off the table by some unseen force and thrown forcibly into LaToya's bedroom, breaking her bedside lamp. When they went over to investigate, they saw a black shadow figure looking at them from an open closet. LaToya yelled for everyone to pack some clothes as quickly as they could and get out of the house. As they were leaving, they watched in horror as "something" lifted the oldest boy, flipped him around, and threw him off the porch. They spent that night at a hotel and the next few days with LaToya's brother, Kevin.

In an interview for the documentary *Demon House*, Kevin stated that the attacks on the children continued at his house.

At night he could hear "whooshing" sounds coming from the bedroom where his youngest nephew slept, as if the boy was being pushed across the floor. Another night, when all three of the kids were in his living room, they "started this weird, evil little chant out of nowhere" in voices unlike any Kevin had heard before. He also recounted a time when he and Rosa were taking the kids to the car and suddenly they started attacking each other like wild animals. When the adults tried to intervene, the children hurled shocking, vulgar insults at them in deep male voices. Never would the children talk that way to their grandmother, Kevin insisted. Never.

On April 19, 2012, LaToya took the children to their family physician, Dr. Geoffrey Onyeukwu, and explained everything that had been happening. She knew she risked being seen as crazy, and possibly having her children taken away, but at this point their safety was her number one concern. Dr. Onyeukwu listened in amazement to LaToya's narrative while the children waited across the hall. "Twenty years, and I've never heard anything like that in my life," he told the *Indy Star*. "I was scared myself when I walked into the room."

The doctor had reason to be wary. As soon as he entered their room, LaToya's sons began cursing at him in raging, demonic voices. Then, in full view of the doctor and other medical staff, the youngest boy was lifted and thrown into the wall by some unseen force. Both boys passed out right after that. Someone at the office called 911 and soon multiple ambulances and police officers were on the scene. Dr. Onyeukwu said of the chaos: "Everybody was...they couldn't figure out exactly what was happening." The boys were taken via ambulance to Methodist Hospital in Gary.

At the hospital, the boys finally woke up. While the older boy, then 9, seemed to be himself and acted rationally, his younger brother screamed and rampaged at those around him. It took five men to hold him down until his frenzy eventually subsided. Staff members then gave physical exams to the children and found them to be healthy and, remarkably, free of bruises or other marks. A psychiatrist examined LaToya and concluded that she, too, was healthy and "of sound mind."

Assisting with the family's evaluation was Department of Child Services (DCS) case manager Valerie Washington. Washington had been called in when DCS received a complaint from an unnamed individual suggesting that LaToya was mentally unwell and abusive toward her children. Her initial interview of the family at the hospital did not go smoothly. While speaking with LaToya, the 7-year-old boy started growling like a predatory animal. His eyes rolled back in his head and then, quickly and without warning, he jumped on top of his brother and locked his hands around the other boy's throat. Adults pried the two boys loose and the interview was suspended.

Later that evening, Washington attempted another interview, this one with just the boys. Their grandmother was present, along with registered nurse Willie Lee Walker. Immediately after settling into the exam room, the 7-year-old looked menacingly into his brother's eyes and began growling again. "It's time to die. I will kill you," he said in an unnatural and deep voice. Then the older boy began head-butting Rosa in the stomach. Rosa grabbed the boy's hands and started praying. What happened next makes this case unique in the annals of paranormal investigations, as there were multiple professional witnesses and an official record of what occurred.

According to Valerie Washington's original DCS report, the older boy flashed a "weird grin" and then proceeded to walk backward up the wall to the ceiling, where he then flipped over Rosa's head and landed perfectly on his feet.

Washington and Walker ran out of the room. "We didn't know what was going on," Walker told the *Indy Star*. "That was crazy. I was like, 'Everybody gotta go.'" When police later asked Washington if maybe the boy had run up the wall like an acrobat, she said, no, the boy "glided backward on the floor, wall and ceiling." Walker confirmed that what they saw was not humanly possible: "He walked up the wall, flipped over her and stood there. There's no way he could've done that . . . . This kid was not himself when he did that."

After Washington and Walker ran out of the room, they told a staff psychiatrist what had just happened. The doctor examined the boy and asked him to repeat his "trick" of walking up the wall again. The boy looked at him strangely. Not only could he not understand what the doctor was asking him to do, but he had no recollection of ever doing it. Since the boy appeared perfectly normal at this point and was suffering from no medical issue or injury, he was allowed to leave with Rosa and his sister. LaToya stayed at the hospital with her youngest son, who was being kept overnight for observation.

The next day was the youngest boy's birthday. He was turning eight and was thrilled when his older siblings and grandmother came back to the hospital to celebrate with a cake and presents. Unfortunately, the celebration did not last long. Valerie Washington informed LaToya that the children would not be going home with her. "All of the children were experiencing spiritual and emotional distress," Washington wrote in her DCS report, which along with other factors led the DCS to take custody of the children without a court order. The family was devastated. "We'd already been through so much and fought so hard for our lives," LaToya told the *Indy Star*. "We made it through together as a team, and they separated us."

The chaplain at Methodist Hospital knew that LaToya and her family needed help beyond what doctors or social workers could provide. On the morning of April 20, 2012, he called Father Michael Maginot, a priest at St. Stephen Martyr Church in Merrillville, with an unusual request. "We need an exorcism," he told Father Maginot, who at the moment was conducting a Bible study. "Can you get down here right away? People ran out of a room after they saw a boy walking backwards up a wall. They called me, and I'm calling you."

In a 2014 interview with the *National Catholic Register (NCR)*, Father Maginot recalled that morning's phone call: "I was not an exorcist, but I knew there needed to be an investigation before anything could be done. There was nothing I could do right then, and I did not want to leave in the middle of the Bible study. I offered to investigate if the family contacted me. They called me the very next day. Their children had been taken away."

On April 22, 2012, Father Maginot met with LaToya and Rosa at the house on Carolina Street. LaToya explained in detail what had been happening in the house and to her and the children. Both she and Rosa assured Father Maginot that neither of them had ever been involved in the occult. Almost as an aside, LaToya told the priest that things seemed to get worse right after her ex-boyfriend visited in March. He gave the boys five dollars each and told them to be good. He told the girl she didn't need anything to be good. Father Maginot began asking more questions about the boyfriend when he was interrupted by a flickering light in the bathroom. He went over to investigate and the flickering suddenly stopped. This happened several times in a row. The light would flicker, the priest would walk over, the flickering would stop. "It must be afraid of me," he quipped.

Ignoring the light, Father Maginot started asking again about LaToya's ex-boyfriend. This time his questioning was interrupted by the Venetian blinds in the kitchen swaying back and forth. Though the air in the house was completely still, the swaying continued in the kitchen window, then spread to the next window, and then the next, until all the blinds in all the rooms were swaying to the same inaudible beat. During this time, wet footprints also materialized in various spots in the living room.

By now several hours had passed, and both women and the priest were fatigued and stressed. LaToya complained of a headache and of feeling strange, as she did at the start of previous possessions. Father Maginot placed a crucifix against her forehead, and she began to convulse. There was no doubt now in the priest's mind that demons were tormenting the Ammons family. He set about doing a major house blessing — praying, reading from the Bible, and sprinkling holy water and blessed salt in each room of the house. Then he told LaToya and Rosa to leave, as it wasn't safe for them there.

The women were able to move in with a relative in Indianapolis, but now LaToya was being plagued with terrible nightmares involving her ex-boyfriend. Father Maginot knew that more had to be done. He petitioned Bishop Dale Melczek for permission to do a formal exorcism on LaToya. In his interview with the *NCR*, Father Maginot speculated that the ex-boyfriend, or someone connected to him, could have put a curse on LaToya using items that belonged to her. He had supposedly once asked LaToya for an article of her underwear as a "souvenir." Around that same time, LaToya had noticed that a few more of her possessions had gone missing, including photographs of her and the kids.

While Father Maginot awaited permission from his bishop, the DCS was still conducting its investigation of the

Ammons family. Less than a week after leaving the Carolina Street house, LaToya and Rosa came back to meet with DCS case manager Valerie Washington to check on the condition of the home. Three police officers accompanied Washington. LaToya refused to go inside, so Rosa led the group through the house, pointing out where different phenomena had occurred and finally leading them down to the basement, where she said she believed the demons originated from. While nothing unusual happened during their inspection of the house, the officers did report some oddities later when they checked their equipment. On one officer's audio recorder, an unknown voice could be heard whispering "hey." And in a photo taken of the basement stairs, a cloudy white image could be seen in the upper right-hand corner, which, when enlarged, appeared to resemble a face. The enlargement also showed a second, green image that looked to observers like a woman.

Gary Police Chief Charles Austin, who was one of the officers present in the house, reported that on the drive back home his car radio was suddenly beset with static and a voice that loudly said, "You in there!" Then, when he arrived home, the garage door refused to open, even though there was no sign of a power outage anywhere. A few days later, the driver's seat in Austin's personal car started moving forward and backward on its own. A mechanic told him the motor on the seat was broken and could have led to an accident. When Chief Austin was interviewed by the *Indy Star*, he said that after multiple visits to the home and interviews with witnesses, he believed the Ammons' claim of paranormal activity. Unfortunately for LaToya, the health and social services workers evaluating her and her children were still skeptical.

After they had been taken into custody by the DCS, the Ammons children had been split up. LaToya's daughter and older son were sent to St. Joseph's Carmelite Home in East Chicago, and her youngest son was sent to Christian Haven in Wheatfield. DCS had argued in its petition for custody that LaToya neglected her children's education by regularly keeping them out of school. LaToya argued back that the children were either sick or had been up all night due to the spirit infestation in their house. The psychologists who evaluated the children concluded otherwise, warning of a "delusional system perpetuated" by LaToya and Rosa that "unduly influenced" the children to a belief in the paranormal. None of the children, however, was found to have an actual psychotic disorder. Recognizing the close bond between LaToya and her children, DCS officials set out a plan to reunite the family once certain objectives were reached, which included, among other things, that the children "not discuss demons and being possessed…"

On May 10, 2012, another meeting at the Carolina house was scheduled. Attending were LaToya, Rosa, Chief Austin, four other police officers, Father Maginot, and DCS case manager Samantha Ilic, who had been called in when Valerie Washington said she wouldn't go back to the house. Father Maginot, thinking there might be evidence of an occult ritual under the stairs in the basement, asked the officers to dig up the dirt there. They unearthed a pink press-on nail, a pin, a lid for a pot, candy wrappers, a small weight, socks with the bottoms cut out, and a pair of women's panties. While that was going on, Ilic noticed a strange liquid on the basement wall that didn't appear to have a source. She described it as slippery yet sticky after touching it with her fingers.

Upstairs, other members of the group discovered a similar oil-like liquid forming on the blinds of one of the bedrooms. Like the basement liquid, this didn't appear to be dripping down from anywhere. Two of the officers cleaned the blinds off with paper towels, and then, to make sure LaToya or Rosa wasn't secretly putting oil on the blinds, they sealed the room and stood guard outside it. After 25 minutes, the officers went back inside the bedroom, puzzled to see that the oil had reappeared. Samantha Ilic had returned upstairs during this time, but she left quickly after her pinky finger suddenly turned white and felt like it was broken. LaToya joined her after she suddenly experienced an excruciating headache and shoulder pain. Father Maginot had seen and heard enough. Though he was still awaiting permission to perform a full exorcism, he was allowed, as all priests are, to conduct a minor exorcism. LaToya, at this point, was willing to try anything and agreed to meet with him in a few days.

Joining LaToya and Father Maginot for the exorcism were two police officers and case manager Ilic. Ilic said afterward that she definitely believed something was happening during the two-hour ritual. "We felt like someone was in the room with you, someone breathing down your neck." The exorcism only granted LaToya a temporary respite. Her nightmares returned, as did other supernatural attacks. Samantha Ilic appeared to be targeted as well by whatever was in that room. Starting a week after the ritual, she experienced a string of accidents that resulted in third-degree burns from a motorcycle, three broken ribs from jet skiing, a broken hand from hitting a table, and a broken ankle from running in flip-flops. "I had friends who wouldn't talk to me because they believed that something had attached itself to me," she said.

On June 1, having finally received permission to conduct a major exorcism, Father Maginot met with LaToya and began the Church's *Rituale Romanum* exorcism rite to engage, and hopefully banish, the diabolic enemy once and for all. Assisting were two police officers, in case there was need for restraint, and a parishioner who was there to respond to the prayers. Somewhat surprisingly, LaToya did not react in any unusual way during the session, though Father Maginot was well aware that demons can play possum. Afterward, he gave LaToya a blessed rosary and was pleased that she showed no discernible aversion to it. Later that evening, however, she called and asked if she had left the rosary at the church. She thought she had put it in her purse but now could not find it. Father Maginot told her they actually had found the rosary—in pieces in the parking lot—right after she drove away. He scheduled a second major exorcism for a week later.

Before they met again, LaToya told Father Maginot that when she had been online once looking for help, she came across a site that listed the names of demons and what each one did. Every time, though, she tried to read about one that seemed to fit what was happening to her and the children, the computer shut down and she would start to feel sick and lightheaded. Father Maginot knew that using a demon's name during an exorcism weakened it, so he printed out the names and descriptions from the website and had LaToya point out the ones she thought could be tormenting her. She chose two. One was known for torturing and hurting children. The other was Beelzebub, lord of the flies.

The demons weren't playing possum anymore. Shortly after gathering these names and preparing for the next session, Father Maginot was pushed off his bike one evening by an unseen assailant, which he believed was an attempt to stop the second exorcism. Undeterred, he met again with LaToya and two assisting police officers. This time, the exorcism had a more dramatic effect. "I went through the rite, and LaToya violently convulsed every time I used one of the two demon names," the priest recalled. "I could see it was getting angrier and angrier." LaToya recalled how she tried to pray along with Father Maginot, but that it increasingly became too painful. "I was hurting all over from the inside out." Eventually, LaToya fell asleep, which is the demon's way of hiding itself from the ritual's effect, according to exorcism lore.

Father Maginot scheduled a third exorcism toward the end of June in order to use the other demon's name. This time he said the rite in Latin, alternating between praising God and condemning the demon. He noted: "LaToya does not know Latin, but she was quiet during the time of praise and convulsed during every condemnation." As the exorcism went on, the priest could tell the demon was weakening. At the closing prayer, LaToya fell asleep. When she awoke, she said she felt good. Father Maginot was thankful for the apparent victory, but because one of the demons hadn't manifested during the rite, he suggested a fourth exorcism in the near future. LaToya, who was now living permanently in Indianapolis with her mother, agreed and said she'd get back to him to schedule it, but it wasn't until October that she actually called. She and the children were fine, she assured him, and she was calling to see if she could get another rosary. She was coming to Gary to attend a hearing for her children.

LaToya never did come by for the rosary, but in November of 2012, she regained custody of her three children. She called their return the happiest day of her life. She also told reporters that the children felt safe in their new home. There were no more instances of demonic voices or activity, and the family now lives without fear. LaToya also called Father Maginot to thank him and let him know that all was well.

Though the official DCS reports credit the agency's intervention and therapy for the family's eventual well-being, LaToya gives credit to a much higher authority. And if people don't believe her, that's fine. As she said in her interview with the *Indy Star*, "When you hear something like this, don't assume it's not real because I've lived it. I know it's real."

Demon House

The house at 3860 Carolina Street in Gary, Indiana, continued to generate unparalleled interest well after the Ammons family had packed up and left. The story in the *Indianapolis Star* about the demonic doings in the house was picked up by numerous news outlets across the world, including the television newsmagazine show *Inside Edition*, which dubbed the house "The Portal to Hell." It was no surprise, then, that the story caught the attention of Zak Bagans, host and executive producer of the Travel Channel's *Ghost Adventures*. Rather than featuring the house on his show, Bagans went one step further: he bought the house.

Bagans intended to produce a documentary about the house, and from 2014 to 2016, he and his crew did the investigative work that resulted in the 2018 film *Demon House*. At the very beginning of the documentary, Bagans warns his viewers that the film is cursed. "Demonologists believe that demons can attach themselves to you through other people, objects, and electronic devices . . . View at your own risk."

The film re-enacts many of the paranormal events that reportedly happened to the Ammons family, including the infamous boy-walking-up-the-wall event. But the primary focus of the film is on the effect the house had on Bagans, his crew members, and other people who had a connection, even peripherally, to the house. The house inspector Bagans hired, for example, nearly had a tree fall on his car while driving home from the inspection and was then choked that night in bed by an unseen attacker. A short time later, he was diagnosed with cancer.

Before he bought the house, Bagans claimed he had a dream of a 12-foot tall goat-man that breathed black smoke into his lungs. Later in the film, one of Bagan's cameramen goes berserk when he claims to see the same demonic figure in the hotel the crew was staying at. Dr. Barry Taff, famous for his investigation of the Doris Bither haunting, spent a day in the house with Bagans measuring geomagnetic levels. That night, he was forced to go to the hospital where he was told his organs were shutting down. (He's since recovered.) And Bagans himself, after spending a night alone in the house, developed permanent eye damage.

These incidents and many others prompted Bagans to have the house demolished in 2016. "Something was inside that house that had the ability to do things that I have never seen before—things that others carrying the highest forms of credibility couldn't explain either," he told the *Indy Star*. "There was something there that was very dark yet highly intelligent and powerful."

According to Father Maginot, who is also featured in the documentary, that dark intelligence is still present. The priest has been open in interviews about his disagreement with Bagans to destroy the house. "I think he could have protected a lot more people [by] owning it, locking it up so people won't mess around with this. Now that it's an open lot, as it mentions in the documentary, people are going there doing séances or whatever . . . Those people are in great danger, and there's no way to really protect [them]."

Father Maginot believes that though the structure is knocked down, a portal still stands, "free for any demon to come through and attack." He routinely has people come to him who have visited the site and are now experiencing strange and frightening things. "They call me because they try and get rid of it themselves, and it won't leave." He cautions all who are tempted to visit the site, or even drive by it, to have some sort of protection with them, such as a religious medal. Better yet, he advises, don't go near it at all. "All you need is curiosity," he says, for a demon to take notice. "Curiosity is an invitation."

Ouija Board Disasters

The following two stories are horrific examples of the chaos and calamity caused time and time again by that most troubling of all occult accoutrements, the Ouija board. They are also examples of a frustrating aspect of deliverance ministry, namely, the acceptance of the demonic oppressor, either because it promises something grand or because it is the easier path to follow. In both cases, not only does this "giving in" lead to the demon's empowerment, making it that much more difficult to vanquish, but brings untold heartbreak to the victim's loved ones, who want nothing more than to see the person they care about set free from their living nightmare.

Henry

Ten-year-old Henry Dennehy was taking his usual route home from school—along a footpath that followed the river for a bit before joining the main road—when he got the sudden urge to veer off the path toward an area of loose sediment and scraggly underbrush. It was a lovely spring day in County Westmeath, Ireland, and he had already passed several joggers and a fisherman or two, so he didn't see any danger in his decision. As he wandered further into the rough, some shiny objects caught his eye, teasing his imagination with thoughts of buried treasure. But as he got closer, it was apparent that there was no treasure, only broken, half-buried junk which had obviously been dumped without any thoughts to environmental or legal concerns. Nonetheless, to Henry the surprise discovery promised hours of exploration and inspection. Perhaps there was *something* of interest amongst all the rubble, and with that possibility in mind, he started poking through the piles.

It wasn't long before he saw something that looked like a game board sticking out of the ground. As he looked at it more closely, he realized it was a Ouija board. Henry was delighted. He had seen this game in movies and had always thought it would be fun to try out. He grabbed the end sticking out and pulled. It was embedded tightly, and as Henry yanked it out something small went flying up in the air. Amazingly, the object didn't fall right back down to the ground. Instead, it remained suspended in the air for several moments before slowly floating down to rest on the board that Henry held in his hands. The object was wooden and triangular with a circle of clear glass in its middle. Though Henry didn't know its proper name, he knew this was the piece of the game that moved around the board when people put their fingers on it.

Though still a little bemused by what had just happened, Henry started brushing the dirt off the board while thinking that it had been a while since he had seen anyone else nearby. He was getting ready to stuff the Ouija in his backpack and head home when something occurred that made the floating planchette seem as ordinary as a chirping cricket. A violent tremor shook the ground, knocking Henry off his feet and the Ouija board out of his hands. The shaking soon stopped, only to be replaced by mournful wails and tortured screams that seemed to be coming from under the earth. Henry tried to get up and run away, but an unseen force pushed him back down and held him in place as a new spectacle unfolded before his eyes. The ground opened up in front of him, revealing a deep, cavern-like space illuminated by rising flames from the bottommost depths. On a throne in the middle of the pit sat a gigantic, hideous figure with blackened leather-like skin and glowing red eyes that looked up directly at Henry. The creature raised its arm, and immediately scores of screeching winged monsters emerged from behind it and flew in a synchronized line of attack right toward the terrified boy. Henry passed out. When he awoke moments later, the vision was gone and he was able to stand up. He quickly gathered up his backpack and ran off as fast as he could.

When Henry arrived home, he nearly knocked his mother over in his haste to run upstairs to his room. "Are you all right?" his mother, Angela, asked. "You're white as a sheet."

"I'm fine," he mumbled as he sidestepped her and rushed to his room.

At dinner, Henry was unusually quiet and picked at his food without really eating anything. Angela asked him again if anything was wrong, but he only nodded his head no and feigned a renewed interest in his plate before finally declaring that he was going to his room to do homework. Less than a minute later, Angela heard an ear-splitting scream and ran out of the kitchen. There, halfway up the stairs, was Henry frozen in place, staring at something at the top of the staircase with a terrified look on his face. "Henry, what is it? There's nothing there," she told him, but the boy remained paralyzed with an expression of fear his mother had never before seen. Just then Henry's younger sister, Kaitlyn, came over and called out his name. When he didn't answer, the girl giggled, clearly thinking they were playing a game. Henry finally responded. He turned and faced his mother and sister with such a look of hatred and contempt that Angela took a step back. She grabbed Kaitlyn's wrist and walked the girl back to the kitchen, instructing her to stay put. When she returned to the stairs, she was relieved to find Henry out of his trance and climbing the rest of the stairs. He told his mother he was going to bed and closed his door behind him.

For the next several days, all appeared to be normal again in the Dennehy household. Henry was once again the affable boy everyone knew, and Angela was close to convincing herself the episode on the stairs was perhaps not as dramatic as she remembered. But then one afternoon, about a week after that incident, Angela heard Kaitlyn crying loudly, followed by Henry shouting, "Get out of here before I kill you!" Angela rushed to the commotion and saw Kaitlyn outside Henry's room holding her left arm. "He twisted my arm *hard*. It really hurts," she said between sobs. Angela confronted Henry about what happened. He shrugged and said, "She was annoying me." Angela was dumbfounded. The two siblings never fought. In fact, she took pride in how well they got along. After much coaxing, Henry promised never to hurt his sister again.

That lasted two days.

Once again, Angela heard screaming from upstairs. This time Henry had punched Kaitlyn in the mouth, loosening one of her baby teeth. Angela was livid, and for the first time ever, she slapped Henry across the face. "What is the matter with you?" she yelled. Instead of tearing up, Henry's face contorted into a twisted mask of malevolence. He balled up his fist and drew back his arm. Angela felt for sure he was going to attack her. But then, like a switch had been turned off, the boy suddenly relaxed, his face went slack, and he murmured, "Sorry," before collapsing on top of his bed.

The next morning at breakfast, an even more concerning event occurred. While sitting at the table, Henry suddenly started to convulse. He fell out of his chair onto the hard floor, where he continued to thrash around violently, his arms and legs jerking about in all directions. Then, as quickly as it started, the convulsions stopped, and Henry lay on his back as rigid as a plank of wood, his eyes glazed over and staring straight at the ceiling. He remained non-responsive even as medics arrived and examined him. It wasn't until he was in the hospital that Henry came out of his trance. He couldn't remember anything that had happened earlier that morning. Doctors tested for every conceivable cause of Henry's seizure: low blood sugar, diabetes, heart disease, even epilepsy. But every test proved negative. Physically, Henry was a healthy ten-year-old boy.

Doctors ordered Henry to stay home from school for a week after he was discharged from the hospital. At home with her son all day, Angela decided the time was right to try to get him to open up about what had happened that day two weeks ago when he raced home after school looking like he had seen a ghost. Certainly the trance he went into on the staircase that same evening and the trance recently in the kitchen were not a coincidence. She sensed that Henry was keeping something from her. She started the conversation by inquiring about Henry's new friend, whom she heard about from Kaitlyn. Henry was not happy that his little sister had not kept his secret.

"Having a friend shouldn't be a secret," Angela said. "So, who is this boy?"

"What boy?" Henry asked in a confused tone.

"Your new friend."

"He isn't a boy. He's a man."

Angela sat back stunned. Thinking that a predator was grooming her son, she felt a wave of nausea move through her. But her fears were soon replaced by incredulity as Henry began telling her about the junk at the river, the Ouija board . . . and his hellish vision.

"The man who was on the throne, that's him. His name is Tyrannus and he was at the top of the stairs that night. He's huge. And sort of scary-looking. I wasn't used to him yet."

"Yet? You mean you've seen him since?"

"Yeah, he talks to me. He tells me things, like what's going to happen in the future. Stuff about history. Cool stuff."

Angela tried to coax more out of her son about Tyrannus, but Henry was adamant he didn't want to talk anymore and retreated to his room. Angela sat on the couch for a while longer, baffled by what she had just heard but also relieved that a pedophile wasn't stalking her son. It seemed that Henry just had a very active imagination. Probably too many horror movies and video games. She went to bed that night hopeful that Henry would pass through this phase soon. She had had enough drama in her life as a domestic abuse survivor and didn't need a new man, even if he was invisible, trying to take control of her family.

* * *

Henry went back to school the following week, but Angela was dismayed to hear from his teachers that his behavior had changed radically—for the worse. She was told he had bullied other students, used foul language, and made rude and threatening remarks to staff members. His behavior had taken a dark turn at home as well. He was coming home later and later from school, always with an excuse, but one October evening when he came home after dark, Angela demanded to know where he had been. No more lies, she warned him. He told her he had been down by the river playing with the Ouija board that was still there. A heated argument ensued until Henry finally ran to his room and slammed the door. An hour or so later, a calmer mother and son reconciled, with Henry promising not to go back to the river.

The next day, Henry did indeed come home at the proper time and seemed to be in a good mood. He even agreed to watch a television show with Kaitlyn after dinner. Angela welcomed these small victories and was feeling pretty good herself when she heard Kaitlyn yell out frantically. Afraid that the bubble had burst and Henry was hurting his sister again, Angela rushed to the living room. Kaitlyn was fine but Henry was not. He was lying on the floor in that same paralyzed position as a few weeks ago. His lips were blue and his eyes were glazed over. Angela immediately ministered to him in an effort to wake him from his stupor. After several frantic minutes, Henry came to, wondering why his mother and sister were crying. Angela called the family doctor.

Dr. Jensen offered to come over but was blunt with Angela. Numerous tests showed there was nothing physically wrong with her son. The problem seemed to be psychological. It could very well stem from the onset of puberty and all the hormonal changes taking place in his body and brain. But he assured her that Henry didn't need medication at this point, just a good therapist. Angela agreed, and the following week Henry began a long-term course of Gestalt psychotherapy, an approach to mental wellness that emphasizes personal responsibility and gaining awareness of the present moment.

Henry's once-a-week treatment sessions seemed to make a difference. Angela was delighted to see her son's sweet-natured personality come back, his grades improve, and his obsession with the Tyrannus character seemingly over with. So it was with great dismay that she received a phone call in the spring informing her that Henry had had a seizure in school. A doctor had seen him, she was told, and he was fine now, but school regulations required that he stay home for a week to fully recuperate.

Thankfully, Angela's neighbor, Marjorie Green, was not only a good friend but was also retired. Marjorie cheerfully undertook "babysitting" duties while Angela went to work that week. No one expected another seizure so soon after the last one, but apparently there were no rules for Henry's condition. The seizure was the same as the others: convulsions followed by a paralyzed body. Marjorie immediately called the doctor and then called Angela. Like the previous seizure, this one didn't last long. Henry was already coming to before help arrived. His only complaint was that he was tired, and after the doctor finished his exam—once again finding nothing medically suspicious—Henry excused himself and went to bed early.

Unlike Angela, Marjorie was a deeply religious person. She had listened to Angela's accounts of Henry's issues and antics over the last year with a concerned mind and a quiet tongue. Until now. She took hold of Angela's hands and told her simply, "Henry needs to see a priest."

"No way," Angela stated firmly. "You know I think that's all a bunch of superstitious nonsense. What possible good could come from Henry seeing a priest?"

"What good has come from seeing doctors and therapists?" Marjorie shot back.

Angela didn't have a reply. Marjorie was right about that, but a *priest*? Good lord! Why not call in a shaman?

"I'll bet you anything the boy's problems came from that Ouija board he found," Marjorie said. "They're bad news, Angela. They let things in."

Things? Angela was too tired to continue this absurd conversation. But she knew Marjorie was sincere and she appreciated her friend's concern. She finally gave in and agreed to meet with Father Thomas Donovan, who Marjorie assured her was a kind and gentle man, as well as a renowned healer. Angela went to bed that night thinking that at this point there was nothing to lose.

* * *

The next day, Angela and Henry made the hour-long trip to the Cistercian monastery where Father Donovan resided. A large, bearded man who had been in the priesthood for over 50 years, Father Donovan was indeed the kindly soul described by Marjorie. He was able to coax from Henry details of recent events that Angela had no idea had even transpired. She was particularly rattled to hear about his stay with her mother. After his third seizure, Angela thought it might be relaxing for him to stay with his grandma for a couple of days. But if anything, he came home more nervous and withdrawn than before. In his conversation with Father Donovan, Henry explained that he didn't sleep well at Grandma's because he kept seeing shadows in his bedroom. Big, black, scary shadows. He also claimed to hear scratching and clawing noises in the walls and ceilings. He resorted to sleeping with the light on, but even that didn't help. Father Donovan then asked Henry about Tyrannus.

"We talk about things. He tells me stuff. He told me what my life would be like when I'm twenty-nine or thirty."

"And what would it be like, son?"

"He said I'd be working at a big desk in a big office and I'd be rich."

"Is that so?"

"Yes, he kept saying I'd have loads of money and power. But—"

Father Donovan waited as Henry looked down in his lap and twisted his hands nervously.

"But I'd have to come over to him," the boy said softly.

"Come over?"

"Do what he wants."

When Father Donovan was done interviewing Henry, he placed a religious relic against the boy's forehead and said a blessing. Then he drew Angela aside and told her that Henry was under attack by an evil force. And it was only going to get worse if he didn't stop cooperating with it. Angela was taken aback by the priest's bluntness. Her son was only a boy. What did he mean by "cooperating"? Father Donovan explained that this Tyrannus creature, who the priest had no doubt was a demon, was seducing Henry with the promise of a fantastic future. The fact that Henry continued to talk with him, with or without the Ouija board, indicated that Henry was succumbing to it.

"He has to resist this thing now or he's going to have a very difficult and painful life, I'm afraid," said the priest. Then he took Angela's hands and looked at her earnestly. "You have to help him fight."

Angela felt overwhelmed. Not having come from a religious background, she was uncomfortable with this talk of demons and battling for her son's soul. But she was also desperate to do something to make Henry better. She agreed to the priest's instructions to have Henry recite special prayers twice a day and to come back in two weeks for another meeting.

For the next few months, Henry faithfully said his prayers and met with Father Donovan on a regular basis. Angela was encouraged that her son hadn't had any more seizures, had not picked any fights with his sister or her, and was not heard "chattering" in his room when he was alone. So when he stopped saying the prayers, first one day, then another, then altogether, she was not too concerned. After all, it appeared that the "thing" had left.

But it had not. And its next manifestation was terrifying. It happened one evening when Henry and Kaitlyn were sitting at the kitchen table together doing homework. Angela was in the next room when she heard Kaitlyn yell, "Mom!

Something's wrong with Henry!" She hurried in to find her son staring off into space with a glassy-eyed expression while his left hand was furiously writing in his notebook. At first glance, it appeared that Henry was writing gibberish. The words, while neatly formed, made no sense at all. It also made no sense that Henry was writing elegantly with his left hand though he was right-handed. When he got to the end of the page—though how he knew this without looking, Angela couldn't fathom—he calmly turned it over and once again began frantically moving his pencil back and forth.

Angela peered more closely this time to what her son was writing. It was no longer gibberish. Spewing forth from Henry's pencil were the most vile words and filthy phrases Angela had ever seen. Interspersed amid the vulgarities were intricate little drawings of occult-like symbols, stars, and sigils. Angela had seen enough. She reached for Henry's wrist but was shocked to discover it was as stiff and hard as an iron pipe. She let go and tried a different tack. She grabbed Henry around the waist and pulled the chair away to unseat him. Incredibly, his body remained in a rigid seated position as if he still had a chair under him, while his writing hand continued to move crazily back and forth in midair. Angela gently pulled him to the ground, where he then collapsed in a faint.

Sick with worry, Angela cradled her son and willed him to wake up, to come back to her as his old self. A few moments later, she breathed a sigh of relief as Henry opened his eyes, looked around, and asked confusedly, "What happened?" Angela helped him up and sat him back down at the table. Then she tore the pages from the notebook that he had written on while in the trance, went out to the living room, and threw them in the fireplace. But when she returned, Henry was staring straight ahead again. Fear and anger took over. Angela grabbed his shoulders and shook him. He broke from his trance and looked directly at her with hate-filled eyes. "F*ck you," he snarled and ran out of the room.

Angela didn't feel right about going back to Father Donovan. It was true that when she and Henry did what he instructed, Henry seemed to be at peace. But it was difficult for them to associate with a religion they weren't familiar with. Though only a nominal Anglican, at least Angela felt like it was *her* religion. She called the local vicar, Reverend Harris, and explained everything that had been happening with Henry from the beginning. He was sympathetic and knew just who to recommend to her: an exorcist by the name of Edward Burton.

* * *

Reverend Burton had interviewed many young people suspected of being demonically oppressed, but none struck him as so bright and well-mannered as Henry. He knew, of course, about Henry's violent outbursts at home and school, but found it hard to imagine the likable, guileless young man in front of him capable of doing such things. As his conversation with Henry went on, however, there was a moment when the boy looked directly into Reverend Burton's eyes and, at that point, the elderly clergyman knew that there was someone, or *something*, else peering at him. The boy's look, Reverend Burton recalled, was "old beyond his years."

The moment passed, and the priest continued his line of questioning. He asked Henry to tell him about the Ouija board. After some initial reluctance, Henry told him he had hidden the board down by the river. He went there two or three times a week to play with it. The man, Tyrannus, was usually with him when he played.

"Tell me about this Tyrannus, Henry."

"He tells me stuff. Like what I'll be when I grow up."

Angela broke in at this point. "Henry, tell the reverend what Tyrannus told you after we made this appointment."

Henry shuffled his feet and hesitated before answering. "He said the Bible was garbage and that I shouldn't read it. And that I shouldn't go to church or even go near one."

"I see. Tell me, Henry, do you agree with him on this?"

"Not really, but he said if I don't do what he says he'll make bad things happen to me. He said he would make me kill myself."

"He can't do that, Henry, if you don't let him. Do you want to be free of him? Free of this evil?"

"Yes," Henry said softly.

Reverend Burton then came over to him holding a Bible and a cross. Henry cowered back and started shaking.

"What's wrong, son?"

"He's laughing, really loud. I can hear him in my head. Tyrannus is laughing at you, Reverend."

"Ignore him. Put your faith in God now, Henry."

Henry continued to shake as Reverend Burton raised his voice and began reciting prayers of deliverance. "In the name of Jesus Christ, I bind you, evil spirit. I strip from you any power over this child." Henry's shaking slowly ceased as the reverend continued with his prayers. The boy sat there with his eyes closed for the remainder of the session. When it was over, he announced that Tyrannus was gone.

"It's up to you now, Henry, to keep him gone. We will say a profession of faith together here, and then I want you to continue saying your prayers at home. Can you do that?"

Henry opened his eyes and nodded. Reverend Burton was happy to see the clear eyes of a ten-year-old boy. He hoped the entity he had glimpsed earlier was indeed gone and would stay away. He just wasn't confident that Henry was committed to the same goal.

"Henry, there is one more thing I want you to do. It's very important. I want you to go down to the river with Reverend Harris and find the Ouija board. Then I want you to burn it. I'll call Reverend Harris in a week to see if that's been done."

Henry nodded and said, "It will be."

* * *

Reverend Burton's concerns about Henry's dependability seemed to be justified. A few days after the deliverance session, Henry and Reverend Harris went down to the river together but saw no sign of the Ouija board. Henry claimed to have no idea what had happened to it. He did say his prayers daily for a few weeks, but only with Angela's coaxing, complaining that they were boring. Besides, he argued, Tyrannus was gone, so he shouldn't have to say them anymore.

Whether or not Henry was actually free of Tyrannus, or any other demonic entity, became increasingly doubtful in Angela's mind. A particularly worrisome episode occurred when Henry stayed overnight at his grandmother's a month or so after the deliverance session. Black shadows, strange noises, and moving objects terrorized not just Henry this time but his grandmother as well, who witnessed an array of manifestations throughout the house. She was so traumatized by these events that she called for an exorcism to be performed on her home.

Any effort by Angela to have Henry meet again with Reverend Burton was met with harsh resistance. Henry grew increasingly sullen and withdrawn, and he made clear he wanted nothing to do with religion, as it was all "stupid." Angela continued to pray for her son but eventually stopped forcing any spiritual course of action on him.

As the years went on, Henry's sullenness turned into full-blown depression. His hatred for anything sacred grew stronger than ever. He became prone to violent outbursts and suicidal thoughts. He went back to seeing a secular therapist, but that, too, he considered a waste of time.

At the time of this writing, it is unknown what happened to Henry as he entered his young adult years. Did he continue his downward spiral and is still plagued by mental and spiritual anguish? Or did he become amazingly successful, a mover and shaker in the business world, as foretold by the mysterious Tyrannus?

The one thing that exorcists of all faiths agree on is that victims of demonic torment must *want* to overthrow their cruel oppressors. Without a true resolution to stop the activity that caused the problem in the first place, and then a further resolution to lead a better life, ideally, a faith-filled life, there is little ministers of deliverance can do, at least of a lasting nature. And the longer the "alliance" of victim and demon continues, the harder it is to unravel the relationship.

For reasons we will never know, Henry seemed to have accepted his demon, or demons. Unfortunately, for some people this is the easier choice to make than resisting and risking a hellish retribution.

It is the choice the demon is counting on.

Sarah

On a cold and rainy November day in 1980, 11-year-old Liam Walsh couldn't get home from school fast enough. He rushed through the door and told his mom that he and his friends had been playing with a do-it-yourself Ouija board they had constructed out of paper and a drinking glass. They had asked the board questions about their futures and actually received answers, he said breathlessly. Could they please, please play it tonight at home?

Sarah Walsh had had a Methodist upbringing and was aware of the admonition against certain occult practices like reading palms and tarot cards. But what harm could a homemade Ouija board cause? It was just a game, she reasoned. Later that evening, she and her three children sat down at the dining room table and began a session with their own paper Ouija board. Much to their delight, they made contact with a spirit that identified itself as a sailor from Admiral Nelson's famous warship, the HMS Victory. After a lengthy question-and-answer session in which the spirit used old English words like "thee" and "thou," Sarah called it a night, promising a second go-around the next day.

The family gathered again the next evening with their paper board, but this time it was a French spirit that came through, claiming his name was JACQUES. Answering questions in simple English with many misspellings, Jacques explained that he had been a blacksmith in the city of Laon and had died during the French Revolution. He had been wandering ever since and was ready to rest. Then Jacques turned his attention directly to Sarah. I WANT TO STAY WITH YOU SARAH, he wrote. Sarah was taken aback, but she was also still skeptical that it was indeed a spirit moving the glass and not one of her children. As if sensing her doubt, the glass then spelled out SARAH SHUT KITCHEN WINDOW. RAIN. To Sarah's bewilderment, the window in the kitchen had blown open, and the stormy weather outside had blown rain all over the counter. From where the family was sitting, none of them could have heard or seen it happen.

Shortly thereafter, Sarah's husband, Justin, came home and, seeing his family gathered around the table, asked what game they were playing. The children excitedly told him they were talking to a spirit and invited him to join them. Justin waved them off as he walked out of the room. "That's a bunch of hogwash," he declared. As soon as Justin was out of sight, the glass began moving again. HE DOES NOT BELIEVE. I WILL COME TONIGHT AS GHOST. While the children were delighted that Jacques was "teasing" about their dad, Sarah had had enough. She told them to go do their homework. Once she was alone, she ripped up the board and threw the pieces into the fireplace, imploring whoever might be listening, "Please just leave us alone. Go away!" As the flames burned and blackened the paper remnants, she noticed that one piece had fallen outside the fire's reach onto the hearth. She picked it up and felt her heart skip a beat when she saw what was written on it: NO.

Later that night in bed, Sarah had a hard time falling asleep. She was troubled, of course, by the evening's Ouija board events, but there was something else, an intangible sense of dread that was making her mind and her heart race. She tried to take comfort in the familiar noises around her—cars going by, the clock ticking, Justin's light snoring—but still couldn't shake the feeling that something—something bad—was about to happen. Soon she heard a noise that wasn't normal: the creak of the doorknob turning. The children never came in unannounced. Even as the door slowly started to open, she knew the intruder was not a child or any other living being. She tried to alert Justin but found, to her horror, that she could neither move nor speak.

But she could hear, and as she lay paralyzed under her bedcovers she heard the heavy tread of booted feet approach. Though she had a direct line of sight on the doorway, she saw no one enter the room. Suddenly a weight descended upon her, a crushing mass that made it hard for her to breathe. She felt a man's unshaven face press against hers, and nearly gagged as the rancid odor of rotting, burning flesh invaded her nostrils. She could taste her tears, though the worst had not yet happened. In the time that followed—Sarah could not tell exactly how long, as her mind was nearly as paralyzed as her body—the phantom fiend sexually assaulted her. She tried to pray but her jumbled thoughts lost track of the words. At some point during the night, she passed out.

When she awoke to the breaking dawn, she knew at once that the "presence" had left. Her body felt light and her mind was clear. She started to think that maybe it had all been a dream. She hoped so, for the alternative was too horrible to consider. Justin stirred next to her a few minutes later. "What's that smell?" he mumbled sleepily. And then Sarah smelled it too, a slight but unmistakable tang of something burnt. Her hopes immediately started to fade. Minutes later they dissolved completely when she looked in the bathroom mirror and saw the bright red rash on the right side of her face, the side her unseen assailant had brushed against mere hours ago. She kept the night's attack to herself, hoping that "Jacques" had by now wandered off to terrorize his next Ouija board victim.

She couldn't have been more wrong.

The phantom rapist came back the next night, and the next, and for weeks and months afterward. It didn't matter if Justin was beside her or not. The same pattern occurred: a sense of dread, the creaking of the door, the fetid breath, the suffocating weight, the unbearable assault. Though she wanted to run and scream at the outset of every attack, she could do neither. That strange paralysis crept over her as soon as the bedroom door started to open, as if the entity could immobilize her from afar. Physical resistance was futile, and when she tried to pray mentally, *he* seemed to know and attacked her more viciously.

Out of shame and fear, Sarah told no one about her tormentor. She convinced herself that if she simply accepted her suffering, it would leave her husband and children alone. Besides, who would believe her? However, Sarah's attempt to "hide" Jacques was not successful. After a few months, odd things began happening around the house. Lights would flicker for no reason; faucets would turn themselves on and off; and small objects would go missing, only to reappear in the most unlikely places. The children complained of hearing mice in the walls, but a pest control check showed no evidence of mice or anything else living behind the plaster. Creaking floorboards were often heard, as well, in rooms where no one was present.

As frequently happens in cases where incremental infestation and regular oppression take place, the paranormal becomes the normal. Sarah's case was no different. Her children eventually got used to the oddities taking place in their home and spoke very little of them. Justin remained clueless as to what was happening to his wife. And Sarah continued to placate Jacques with her silent acquiescence to his molestations. Though she had once been a church-going believer, Sarah had finally given up on both public worship and private prayer. She had learned the hard way that any attempts at piety on her part enraged her infernal foe and resulted in worse attacks than usual. But if she ignored her faith, Jacques would often leave her alone for periods. For years this diabolical arrangement was the Walsh family's existence.

Then one night in 1991, something changed. Jacques tried to kill her. Looking back at the event during an interview, Sarah said this was the night she fully realized that Jacques was not a callous ghost or an evil spirit but was indeed a demon and that he intended to take full possession of her, even if that meant her bodily death. The nightly ritual started like all the others—the terrible odor, the paralyzing weight, the stubbled cheek—but quickly turned into a fight for survival. A phantom hand grasped Sarah's throat and squeezed so tightly she thought her neck would snap. Barely able to breathe, she turned in desperation to her instinctual faith, and with every ounce of strength gasped, "In the name of Jesus Christ, get out!" The hand on her throat released its grip and the weight on her body receded. Jacques was gone. For now. But from past experience, Sarah knew he'd be back, and with a vengeance.

It wasn't even an hour before Sarah heard a zooming noise rapidly approaching her bed. The attack was fast and fierce. A massive weight greater than she had ever experienced before fell upon her. She had no doubt the demon was trying to crush her to death. She turned again to God: "Dear Lord, don't let me die," she pleaded. And then, the words that had worked earlier: "In the name of Jesus Christ, get out!" The weight lifted, and Sarah sat up, gasping for breath and waiting for another attack. When none came, she reached over and turned on the bedside lamp and immediately regretted doing so. Clearly exposed in the light was a shapeless, pulsating black cloud at the end of her bed. It radiated evil so intensely that Sarah thought she would die of terror. Then a voice emanated from it, but it wasn't the voice of a Frenchman or any other once-human being. It was coarse, grating, and angry. "No talking! Go to sleep!" it commanded. Sarah instantly fell asleep, the demon's power over her still chillingly evident.

When she awoke the next morning, Sarah felt something she hadn't felt for ages: hope. She had defied the demon Jacques last night and survived. It hadn't been easy, and she knew the road ahead would be extremely difficult, but she was ready to fight. She was done letting this fiend control her. She would come out in the open and drag Jacques with her. She went first to her sister, Marion, who amongst all the family members was the most devout. After hearing Sarah's incredible story, Marion told her she needed an exorcist. She also gave her a framed painting of Christ to hang in her bedroom.

The solution seemed simple enough: find an exorcist. But the actual task proved difficult. Every minister Sarah talked to listened with sympathy but ultimately conceded that they couldn't help. Sarah began to think they were just too afraid. As she continued her search, Jacques went on a counterattack. Paranormal activity in the house increased in frequency and intensity. Sarah would often be awakened by a dog barking, though the family didn't own any pets. If not a barking dog, a man's mocking, evil laugh would bring her out of sleep. Only Sarah heard these things, as neither Justin nor their children ever claimed to be bothered in this manner. One night when Justin was working a late shift, Sarah was awakened by the familiar, ominous laughter. As she was used to doing, she looked over to Marion's picture of Christ for comfort. But this night she felt little peace. Instead, she watched in horror as invisible hands lifted the painting from its hooks and threw it down to the ground, smashing it to pieces.

As much as Sarah wanted to come completely clean to her family about what had been happening to her for more than a decade, she still could not confess everything. Her story was simply too outrageous and shameful to be believed. Plus, she still hadn't been able to find an exorcist, and without some sort of supernatural protection, she feared retaliation against those she loved. But when Jacques changed the ground rules in 1993 by attacking her oldest child, Liam, Sarah stopped playing the demon's game for good.

The incident occurred when Liam was tasked with watching over the house while Sarah, Justin, and the younger children went on vacation. A young man of 24 now, Liam looked forward to having the run of the house for a few days. Maybe he'd even have some friends over. His plans quickly changed. Liam recalled how on his first night alone in the house, an extreme cold settled in, despite it being the middle of summer and regardless of how high he set the thermostat. The second night, he decided to sleep in his parents' bedroom, hoping it would be warmer. He was getting ready for bed when he heard something fall to the ground behind him. He turned and saw a small wooden cross on the floor, which apparently had come loose from its nail on the wall. But when he went to hang it back up, he noticed that the nail was still firmly in the wall and at an angle that should have held the cross securely. Not thinking too much more of it, he climbed into bed.

He had just started to fall asleep when he heard a creaking noise to the side of him. He opened his eyes fully, just in time to see his mother's wardrobe moving on its own toward him. As the towering piece of furniture inched its way closer, Liam untangled himself from the bedcovers and rolled over to the far side of the bed as quickly as he could. And not a second too soon. With a final creak and groan, the wardrobe tipped over and came crashing down on the side of the bed where Liam had been just moments ago. Liam ran from the room and spent the rest of the week at a friend's house.

When Sarah heard what had happened, she gathered the family together and revealed her torturous oppression by the demon calling itself Jacques, saving the most intimate details for her husband's ears only. Justin couldn't believe he had been present during the attacks on his wife all those years without a clue as to what was happening. He could barely remember the Ouija board session that had started it all. But he was now as firmly committed to driving it from their lives as was Sarah. Together they renewed the search for an exorcist, and this time they were successful. Word of mouth led them to an elderly Anglican priest with an impressive track record in demonic deliverance.

Canon John Westmore gave Sarah his full attention as she related her story over the phone. Compassionate and understanding, he agreed at once to come to the house. He warned her, though, that the demon might ramp up its activities before he could get there, knowing that plans had been made to cast it out.

And indeed it did. When the family awoke the next morning, they were subjected to a legion of paranormal phenomena, the worst of which was a stench so revolting it made Sarah and Justin rush outside and vomit. Books were pushed off their shelves, teacups sailed through the air, and electrical appliances either started up by themselves or refused to come on at all. At one point, Sarah was forced to stop vacuuming because the noises coming from the vacuum's motor made her think it was about to explode.

That evening, Canon Westmore and two assistants arrived at the Walsh home. Immediately upon entering, the clergyman sensed that something was wrong in the house. There was a peculiarity to the air; it was cold and foul-smelling, heavy and hostile. From everything Sarah had told him, including the most recent ruckus from Jacques, Canon Westmore expected a battle, but this early manifestation of the demon's presence surprised him a little. "It was worse than I imagined," he recalled a few years later in an interview. "These cases, where the demon has lived in the house and oppressed someone for so long, are always difficult. It feels it has the right to stay put."

The exorcist got to work. He set up a makeshift altar and laid out the sacred objects needed for the celebration of the Eucharist. Then he heard the private confessions of all the family members. This helped him to determine if the demon had taken over only the home or an actual person, as those who are truly possessed will find confessing quite upsetting if not intolerable. Thankfully, Sarah did not fall into this category. She was more than determined to reject all evil and recommit her life to God. Now knowing the situation he was dealing with, Canon Westmore began the ritual.

As the clergyman led the little group in prayer, the wind outside began to howl. As he distributed the communion bread and wine, it howled even more. When he raised his hands to heaven and called upon the power of Christ to bind the evil in the house, the wind shrieked like a tortured animal and shook the house like a horde of crazed barbarians. The overhead lights began to flicker and sway back and forth. The Walshes maintained their composures as best they could, taking their cues from the calm and unwavering demeanors of Canon Westmore and his assistants.

Suddenly the lights went out and the room was enveloped in darkness, save for the small area of candlelight around the altar. Canon Westmore continued reciting the prayers from his ritual book. A door to an adjoining room began to slowly open. One of the assistants calmly went over and closed it. A tremendous gust of wind hit the house and blew open a window. Again, an assistant went over and closed it. Sarah wasn't sure if it was her imagination or not, but at this point she thought she felt the air "lighten." She hoped and prayed it meant something was leaving. The clergyman next sprinkled holy water in all corners of the room. Then he walked throughout the house, blessing all the other rooms with holy water.

By now, everyone was feeling a difference in the air. Where before there had been a sense of danger and despair, now there was a feeling of peace. Canon Westmore ended the service with prayers of thanksgiving and declared to the relieved family that the demon had departed.

Before he left, Canon Westmore asked Sarah if she would come into the kitchen for a moment. "I noticed as I was making my rounds this open window. Is this the same one—?" Sarah was speechless. She knew for a fact she had closed and locked the window before the exorcism team arrived. The weather forecast had been calling for rain. But now it had blown open by itself as it had all those years ago when she first played with the Ouija board. She nodded mutely. The priest chuckled as he walked over and closed it. "Nothing to fear, my dear. It appears our friend Jacques has left the building."

In Closing

The world is a dangerous place, with attacks on our minds, bodies, and spirits coming fast, frequently, and from every direction. Just a quick look at the morning headlines may make us want to curl back up in bed and pull the covers over our heads. That solution may keep out the earthly problems, but what of the non-earthly? As we've seen in the accounts in this book, there is no place to run and hide when an evil spirit takes an interest in you.

Though that sentiment may make you shudder and give in to despair, don't let it. Most of us will never experience an extraordinary demonic attack. And for those that do, there are ways to fight back. But the first and foremost guideline to follow is this: don't invite the enemy in. Don't join a satanic cult, don't visit a fortune teller, don't play with Ouija boards. Stay away from the occult, period. Avoid relationships with people who are involved in the occult. As often happens, their "attachments" could likely become yours.

By the same token, be wary of paranormal investigations and "ghost hunting." These activities are basically necromancy, in that they are attempts to make the dead manifest and communicate. But instead of "ghosts" coming through, what often happens is demons will show up instead. Some exorcists estimate that up to twenty-five percent of the demonic oppression cases they deal with come from paranormal investigating. And though it is rarely admitted on the shows, many of the participants in television ghost hunting series become afflicted with demonic troubles themselves.

Finally, don't attract evil to yourself by engaging in evil. Stay away from crime, drugs, pornography, and other negative lifestyle choices. Do not let violence, abuse, or dark obsessions rule your household. Be positive. Be life-affirming. If you belong to a church, continue in your faith tradition. If you don't, consider looking into it. Demons abide by religious commands. That should tell us something.

But what if, through no fault of your own, you find yourself under demonic attack? Perhaps you moved into a house that was already infested. Maybe someone put a curse on you. Or you unknowingly brought a cursed object or invited a possessed person into your home.

First and foremost, don't make it worse. Performing a self-styled "exorcism" with items picked up from the local New Age shop or sprinkling holy water all over without any faith behind your actions will only make the entity more empowered and may intensify its malicious activity. Similarly, avoid paying for a psychic, medium, or shaman to disperse the "negative energy." Fighting the occult with the occult is always risky and often dangerous. These actions may seem to work at first, but more often than not the demons come back, worse than before.

Get help, yes, but only from someone who has the knowledge, training, and authority to properly deal with the demonic. Even then, be prepared for an often lengthy and frustrating process. Demons are peculiarly legalistic and will fight hard to retain their "rights" to a person, place, or thing. As we've seen in the preceding stories, it oftentimes takes multiple house blessings, deliverance prayers, and full-on exorcisms to completely banish the infernal squatters.

The good news? Good always wins over evil in the end. *If* good is truly desired, that is. Some people do spend the better part of their lives under demonic subjugation, but that is almost always by choice. Most people can free themselves of a demon's grasp by renouncing the evil that attracted it, resolving to live a good life, and cooperating with those who truly want to help. There are exceptions, people that seem to suffer the scourge of the diabolic no matter what they do. Such cases, like so much in the paranormal world, remain a puzzle.

What is certain is that demons are real and that they are bent on misleading and harming us. While it's advisable not to become obsessed or paranoid over them, it is wise to take a sober account of their existence and activities, lest we become victims to them ourselves.

> *"There isn't a demon hiding under every rock — just every other one."*

– Fr. Chad Ripperger, exorcist

Selected Bibliography

Armstrong, Patti Maguire. "Parish Priest Aids Family in Fight Against Demons." *National Catholic Register*, February 11, 2014.

Baines, Wesley. "Interview With an Exorcist." *Beliefnet.com*.

Blai, Adam. *Hauntings, Possessions, and Exorcisms*. Emmaus Road Publishing, 2017.

"Chilling: Inside a Demon House." *Fox 8 News Cleveland*, April 28, 2014.

Clarkson, Michael. *The Poltergeist Phenomenon: An In-depth Investigation Into Floating Beds, Smashing Glass, and Other Unexplained Disturbances*. The Career Press, 2011.

Cranmer, Bob, and Erica Manfred. *The Demon of Brownsville Road*. Berkley, 2014.

Demon House. Directed by Zak Bagans. Freestyle Releasing, 2018.

Edwards, Frank. *Stranger Than Science*. Random House Publishing, 1973.

Fortea, Antonio. *Interview With An Exorcist*. Ascension Press, 2006.

Gallagher, Richard. *Demonic Foes: My Twenty-Five Years as a Psychiatrist Investigating Possessions, Diabolic Attacks, and the Paranormal*. HarperOne, 2020.

Kiely, David and Christina McKenna. *The Dark Sacrament: True Stories of Modern-Day Demon Possession and Exorcism*. HarperCollins Publishing, 2007.

Kwiatkowski, Marisa. "The Exorcisms of Latoya Ammons." *IndyStar*, January 25, 2014.

"Mayor to Ask Archbishop to Exorcise Draculas." *The Sydney Morning Herald*, May 20, 1953.

Ortega, Xavier. "The Entity: An Interview with Doris Bither's Son." *GhostTheory.com*, May 18, 2009.

Ortiz, Anna. "Portal to Hell Lingers in Region, Priest Says." *nwitimes.com*, September 25, 2020.

Page, Debra. "Elemental Haunting." *Pacificparanormal.com*.

Romero, Jesse. *The Devil in the City of Angels: My Encounters With the Diabolical*. Tan Books, 2019.

Sarchie, Ralph and Lisa Collier Cool. *Beware the Night*. St. Martin's Press, 2001.

Sawyer, J.W. *Deliver Us From Evil*. OmniMedia Publishing, 2009.

Syquia, Jose Francisco C. *Exorcism: Encounters with the Paranormal and the Occult*. Shepherd's Voice Publications, 2006.

Taff, Barry. "The Real Entity Case." *Barrytaff.net*, August 7, 2011.

Thurston, Herbert. *Ghosts and Poltergeists*. Henry Regnery Company, 1954.

Yamsuan, Cathy. "Demonic Texts: The Enemy Can Use Technology, Says Exorcist." *Philippine Daily Inquirer*, November 1, 2020.

Yamsuan, Cathy. "Treehouse of the Spirits." *Philippine Daily Inquirer*, October 28, 2018.

Zaffis, John. *Shadows of the Dark*. iUniverse, 2004.

About the Author

John Harker is a freelance journalist and ghostwriter who's been writing and publishing since the 1990s. His personal encounters with unexplainable phenomena have inspired him to explore strange, dark, and disturbing topics in both non-fiction and fiction. He lives with his family in eastern Washington, where the ghosts are dry and dusty.

Visit John's website, johnharkerbooks.com, for updates on book releases, paranormal news, and other information.

Also by John Harker

Monsters and Maniacs: True Tales of Mystery and Horror

*Evil Unleashed: True Tales of Spells Gone to Hell
and Other Occult Disasters*

Demonic Dolls: True Tales of Terrible Toys

Ouija Board Nightmares: Terrifying True Tales

Ouija Board Nightmares 2: More True Tales of Terror

Compendiums

Ouija Board Nightmares: The Complete Collection

True Tales Trilogy: Nightmarish Accounts of Paranormal Activity

Ingram Content Group UK Ltd.
Milton Keynes UK
UKHW021122180423
420361UK00014B/909